# PRESENTING YOURSELF
# WITH IMPACT

CW00419161

# PRESENTING YOURSELF
WITH
# IMPACT
AT WORK

## GILL GRAVES

bookshaker

First Published in Great Britain 2010
by www.BookShaker.com

*For Dad. My inspiration and true north.*

# PRAISE

*"In Presenting Yourself With Impact, Gill Graves, not only provides an excellent framework for any business leader or manager interested in improving their ability to deliver key messages and engage people effectively; it is also an excellent introduction for anyone, in any walk of life, who simply wants to improve their ability to communicate and be understood by other people."*
Andrew Brodie, Head of HR, Faccenda Group

*"Gill's book is convincing evidence that we all have the skills within us we need to succeed - we just need to know how to harness the resources available and channel them appropriately. Removing limiting beliefs we never knew we held, changing a few habitual words we use regularly when we speak, thinking through how to reach our desired audience. Individually small changes, but together the impact on the end performance is dramatic and lasting."*
Kate Markham, Head of Commercial Development, Vodafone

*"Presentation skills are an essential element in every professional's toolkit, yet many people struggle to present themselves and their message effectively. Gill Graves's approach instills confidence and helps individuals make an impact with clients, customers and colleagues."*
Anne Howells, Director, Learning & Teaching Solutions, The Open University

*"Gill is probably regretting to this day that she armed me with the skills to be able to present 'opportunities' to her to help me with my projects in such a way she can't say no! She is the best coach and mentor I have ever worked with and I use the skills and techniques she has taught me every day. These skills have become especially important in my new job working with the blind and partially sighted."*
Tracy Bracher, District Fundraiser, Guide Dogs for the Blind

*"Gill's coaching has significantly increased my personal impact - I'm much more self aware, delivering an impact that I control, and getting positive outcomes - for me and for others. Gill coaches with a good blend of carrot and stick; communicates with knowledge, common sense and empathy; and guides me to find my own solutions to improve my personal performance. She writes with the same no-nonsense style of advice and encouragement; and if you get from her book only half of what I get from working with her in person, then you'll still be onto a winner and presenting yourself with impact in no time!"*

Adrian Griffiths, Head of Mental Health & Continuing Healthcare Finance, NHS Birmingham East & North

*"I attended the Presenting Yourself With Impact course in 2004 and immediately found that it took me through my comfort zone and beyond...thus opening up an amazing new world of communications capabilities, which were already embedded in me but which otherwise would never have seen the light of day. This result for me has been profound, both in personal and professional terms and now I would not dream of embarking on a new venture - or expecting others to follow me on it - without going through my 'pre-flight checklist' of the things which I have learned and regularly apply from Presenting Yourself With Impact."*

James Moberly, Global Business Development, Vodafone

*"As an interim executive I frequently need to supplement my skills with those that I simply do not possess. I don't have the time or luxury to be able to afford a failure: it has to work first time. This is the way it is with Gill Graves and the enthusiasm, skill and indeed impact she has when presenting her subject comes across forcefully in this book. I am sure that there will be many reading this extremely helpful text who will want to see Gill in action: I can thoroughly recommend it."*

Dr Terry Summers, Interim Executive

"I have known Gill for many years. We first worked together when I was at Vodafone working on the design of the 'Art and Science of Leadership' strategy. Since then Gill has helped me at BAE Systems and also at LexisNexis. We have worked together on the coaching of high potential executives and, in particular, on the need to demonstrate a positive high impact in presentations. Gill has a really rounded and experienced view on both the behavioural and the psychological processes that need to be mastered in order to be successful. This book captures much of her knowledge in this area and will prove to be a really valuable and practical tool for managers and leaders."
Rob Shorrick, HR Director

# CONTENTS

# ACKNOWLEDGEMENTS

A special thank you to my husband Colin, for initially posing the question, "So when's the book coming out?" and for his constant support, research, proof reading and belief in me.

In addition, there are so many family, friends, mentors, clients and colleagues to thank. Many of them appear in this book – albeit under various aliases! You know who you are and a big thank you for your support and inspiration.

This book could not have been written without the many clients who have attended my workshops or been coached by me. Thank you for all the real life stories you have provided and for enriching my work and life.

My gratitude to Tracy for co-presenting on my Presenting Yourself with Impact workshop on so many occasions and for providing many of the mind and body exercises in Chapter Seven.

To Debbie and Joe at Bookshaker for their support and enthusiasm.

# FOREWORD

I am one of the lucky ones. I have seen Gill at work in delivering her workshops, having taught alongside her on a major programme for mid-career executives being fast-tracked to board-level positions. Simply put, Gill is very good at what she does.

This book, for the first time, captures key features of her teaching. It is not a scholarly book, nor is it intended to be. As Gill herself writes, it is intended as "a field manual, a practical text with real life examples and exercises you can practise, either on your own or with colleagues". The exercises are tried and tested – and they work.

If only I had known some of the things included here when I made my first presentations, I might have made more impact and avoided some rather embarrassing situations: arriving underdressed, mumbling the ends of my sentences, being unclear of where I wanted to go, using inappropriate metaphors or jokes that fell flat, being more concerned with the impression I tried to create rather than the story I wanted to tell, prizing my performance over the learning of others … memories that make me cringe even now.

Realizing full well that this page stands in the way of you delving into the main text, let me leave you with some memorable lines by Thom Bishop:

> *If we want to see where we went wrong*
> *We needn't look too far,*
> *For where we'll be and where we've been*
> *Is always where we are.*
> *And everything that comes your way*
> *Is something you once gave,*
> *Somebody feels the water*
> *Every time you make a wave.**

Enjoy this book. Use it. It helps.

**Mark de Rond, Judge Business School, Cambridge.**

Mark is the author of several books including the best seller: *The Last Amateurs: To Hell And Back With The Cambridge Boat Race Crew.*

* From "Truth in Comedy" by Charna Halpern, Del Close and Kim Johnson, 1994, Colorado: Meriwether Publishing Ltd., p.11

# PREFACE

When I first met Gill more than 15 years ago, she was a client of mine. Gill was, at that time, the European Human Resources Director of a leading high technology company. The world of international human resources management and leadership, with all its incredible complexity and diversity is not for the faint of heart. And Gill, being Gill, handled it all with keen insight, depth of intelligence, compassion, enormous tact of course, grace and her characteristic good humour and wicked wit! We clicked immediately, and a relationship that I treasure today, was born.

When I think of Gill in the context of the initial "impact" she had on me, and the impression she made, I think of her tremendous energy, drive for excellence, her no-nonsense and clear competence, her courage, her warmth and her steady and inspiring presence. Those "first impressions" have stood the test of time—more than 15 years---and as I have watched Gill build her business and develop ever greater strengths and areas of expertise, what I simply see is Gill becoming more and more her best self. Gill is a "pro", she is the "real deal", truly authentic in all she does and I believe that all of us who have the pleasure of working with her, and the privilege of calling her a friend, recognize that in her.

While Gill brings great depth, knowledge, expertise and credibility to all she does, one of Gill's most endearing and enduring qualities is never taking herself too seriously. She has the courage, the confidence and the curiosity to be ever stretching and challenging herself. This book, in which Gill shares some of her insights, principles and perspectives, is a perfect example of that, and it is a gift to us all. Thanks, Gill!

**Christine Crossman, Christine Crossman Consulting.**
Christine is an international HRD Consultant based in Ottawa, Canada.

# INTRODUCTION

Six years ago I was developing a workshop for my largest client and was struggling to choose a name for it. The workshop was all about how to have an impact on others in formal and informal settings – the kind of impact you actively want to make. I felt the word 'impact' had to feature in the title, but wanted to avoid 'presentations' in case people associated it principally with PowerPoint. I wanted to discourage participants from relying on PowerPoint to deliver their message.

Six years on, *Presenting Yourself with Impact* is our most popular programme and we run in-house versions of it for a number of our clients. It remains my favourite programme. It is amazing how subtle differences – standing upright, using impactful words, letting go of filler words – can make such a big and positive difference so quickly.

Participants are delighted with the progress they have made and amazed by the change they have seen in others. Just last week one told me he had been really looking forward to attending the workshop as he had seen a massive difference in one of his colleagues who had attended the same workshop four months earlier. If he could experience just *some* of that improvement himself, he would be thrilled.

Over six years the workshop has changed, of course, although the core content and the intent remain the same. The most significant development is the inclusion of the Mind and Body session on the second morning for which I am indebted to my friend and colleague, Tracy. The content was developed for use in a workshop with several participants, but I now use a lot of the tools and techniques individually with my coaching clients, some of whom have suggested I write this book.

This therefore is a field manual, a practical text with real life examples and exercises you can practise, either on your own or with colleagues. Each chapter combines theory, real life examples and stories taken from my own experience, as well as the exercises. You can work through the content in a logical way, ending with a final chapter on putting it all together or you can also dip into the chapters in any order, depending on where you want to focus your attention and learning.

The flow of chapters is as follows:

### One – Outcome-Based Communication

This chapter focuses on the importance of knowing your outcome before you start, the message you want to get across to your audience, and how to present this in a memorable way.

### Two – Enabling and Limiting Beliefs

Most books on presentation skills focus on the acquisition of new skills and behaviour. This chapter explores how, if we do not challenge some of the beliefs we have about ourselves as presenters, our chances of embracing and using our new skills are severely reduced.

### Three – Building Rapport

'Rapport' is one of those words that we use without thinking about its real meaning. What does it mean to be in rapport with someone? How do we know we have rapport? It is so much easier to get people to buy into our message if we have some level of rapport with them. This chapter seeks to answer these questions and explores how we can set about building rapport with our audience.

## Four – Engaging The Senses

Here we explore the different ways in which people take in and process information, going on to analyse how we can use this knowledge to make sure we engage all the senses when presenting our message both in the language and medium we choose.

## Five – Language Of Influence

How can we use language to positively influence our message? We look at how the use of some everyday words and expressions can reduce our overall impact. We also look at words and language patterns which, if used sparingly, can create a positive impression on our audience and get them into a 'yes' way of thinking.

## Six – Creating A Resourceful State

Using the technique of anchoring, we can create a resourceful state for ourselves, be it confidence, energy, calm, which we can access when we need it, and use this state to our advantage.

## Seven – Mind and Body

A highly practical chapter focusing on how we can increase the positive impact we have non-verbally (posture and gestures) and verbally (volume, pitch, breathing and tonality). It includes a series of short exercises to practise, either on your own or with colleagues.

## Eight – Stepping into Your Audience's Shoes

Here we explore one of the key skills of great negotiators/influencers/presenters – the ability to put yourself in someone else's shoes and experience the world through their senses. We will focus on how we can use this technique to tailor our message, and how we present it to our specific audience.

## Nine – Getting Prepared

Hints and tips for preparing and delivering a formal presentation to a large audience: choosing your presentation medium, structuring your message, thinking about your venue, handling questions.

## Ten – Having a Go!

This brings everything together and provides you with some final thoughts about getting started, preparation and rehearsal, reflecting on your experiences and extracting the learning.

# CHAPTER ONE

# OUTCOME-BASED COMMUNICATION

At the start of a workshop or coaching session on presentation skills I ask participants to introduce themselves by answering the following three questions:

1. Why are you here (answering this in the positive)?

2. What *specifically* do you want to achieve?

3. How will you know you have been successful? In particular what will you be seeing, hearing and feeling when you are successful?

You may want to take a moment and answer these questions for yourself in relation to the reading of this book.

1.

2.

3.

## WHY AM I HERE?

I asked four people why they wanted to attend a modular leadership programme.

This is what they said:

1. "I'm not sure exactly. My boss attended this programme a couple of years ago and he's always going on about how great it is and how it would be useful for me. So I decided to apply – partly to keep him quiet but I've got an open mind. How useful will it be for me? Time will tell ..."

2. "I tried to get on this programme last year but it was full so I was determined to be successful this year. It sounds great – really different and stretching you out of your comfort zone. Not sure quite what I'll get out of it but I'm a big believer that you always learn something!"

3. "I've been with this organisation for eight years and in my current role for five years. I feel stuck in a rut and I don't know how to get out of it. I don't want to be doing this job for the rest of my working life. I think this programme will help with my career development."

4. "I'm ready to take the next step from functional head to a leader within the business. I see this programme as being a great vehicle for expanding my horizons, giving me some new tools and for networking possibilities. I particularly want to improve my presentation style – I'm comfortable giving presentations but I feel I lack impact. I believe this programme will give me some useful tools and tips to improve my overall impact. I'll know I've been successful when I deliver a presentation to a senior

audience and they all look interested and engaged throughout, I get very few questions or ones which build on my presentation and I feel really confident at the end – as if I've really nailed this one!"

What impact does each explanation have on you?

Let us look at my reasons for asking each of the three questions.

1. Why are you here (answering this in the positive)?

2. What specifically do you want to achieve?

3. How will you know you have been successful? In particular what will you be seeing, hearing and feeling when you are successful?

## NEURO LINGUISTIC PROGRAMMING

Much of the work I do with presentation skills includes Neuro Linguistic Programming (NLP) tools and techniques. Often referred to as "the study of excellence" NLP is a way of decoding and reproducing what works in thinking, language and behaviour.

NLP stands for:

- **Neuro –** The way we use our minds and physiology.
- **Linguistic –** The way we use language to make sense of experience.
- **Programming –** How we code our experience; our patterns for responding.

When I am working with individuals or groups I sometimes hear expressions such as "Yes, but aren't great presenters born not made" and "Aren't some people just natural presenters whereas others aren't?" I believe there is an element of truth in these sentiments and some people have innate personality traits which help them be great presenters. However, that is certainly not the whole story.

NLP challenges the concept of skills being purely innate. Indeed it goes further by believing that, if we can discover the structure of what a skilful person does in terms of behaviour, skills, values/beliefs, others can learn this same skill. In short NLP sets out to understand what it is that makes the difference between average results and excellence.

For a number of years now I have enjoyed running. Nothing too strenuous, a few miles two or three times a week and the odd 5k or 10k race. I have slowly improved my stamina and race times although I have not put too much effort into doing so. However, if I really wanted to develop as a runner and, for example, challenge myself to run a marathon, I could go and spend some time with a serious runner. I could find out not only how they train, but also about their diet and sleep regime as well as what they believe about themselves as a runner. If I then took their whole running strategy and adopted it myself my running would almost certainly improve. This principle is called **modelling** and can be applied to the development of a wide range of skills and techniques.

Returning to the questions I posed at the start of this chapter these all relate to aspects of something I refer to as Outcome-Based Communication. In *Influencing with Integrity*, Genie Z Laborde states,

*"Communicating without a desired outcome is like travelling without a destination. You may end up in a place you really enjoy, or you may not. Enjoying your trip is a perfectly good outcome; ending up at the destination you want is also productive."*

The elements of Outcome-Based Communication are:

- Be Specific
- Use Positive Language
- Define Your Success Criteria
- Own Your Own Messages

## BE SPECIFIC

Good communicators send clear messages by being specific about what they want and, where possible, give the facts to support what they are saying. For example, skilled communicators will say "Please do this by 3 pm on Tuesday" rather than use a vague imprecise phrase such as "Please do this as soon as possible".

Look back at the notes you have just made about your own outcomes. Take a moment to analyse your answer. How specific was it? How can you make it more specific?

A number of years ago I was using this exercise in a workshop and one of the participants said her reason for being there was to "Improve her communication skills".

Communication skills is a huge area and so I asked her what part of communication skills she wanted to improve? She said her presentation skills. I asked her to tell me more and, after a brief exchange of questions and answers she came to the conclusion that it was presenting to senior audiences that was the biggest challenge for her. Once a month she had to present to a senior board and she wanted to have more confidence and impact with this group. With other forms of presentation she felt comfortable and confident. Having created a specific goal for herself she was then able to work on tools and techniques to increase her impact with her target audience throughout the remainder of the workshop.

## USE POSITIVE LANGUAGE

Our unconscious mind does not recognise negatives and either deletes or ignores these. For example, what happens if I ask you NOT to think of fish? The first thing that immediately jumps into your mind is a picture of a fish. It is impossible not to think of fish! If you still doubt me, think about what a child will invariably do when you tell them NOT to touch something!

If you tell a person what you do *not* want, they have to take on board what you have said and then reverse the meaning. So, if we say "I don't want to do X" the listener has to (a) think about wanting to do X and then (b) think about what it means not to want to do X.

Consequently it is more effective to get into the habit of directly asking for what we do want to happen rather than what we want to avoid. For example, "I would like to start this meeting on time" rather than "I don't want to be late starting", "remember to agree the delivery schedule" rather than "don't forget to finalise the delivery requirements".

Again, take a moment and look at the outcomes that you have written down. Have you said what you want in positive language or have you stated what you want to avoid? For example, "I don't want to be nervous when I am presenting". If you have stated what you don't want, flip in around into the positive: what would you like instead?

## MY SUCCESS CRITERIA – SEE/HEAR/FEEL

Cast your mind back to the last Olympic Games. It is the Men's 100 metres final and the athletes are all poised on the starting line. All of these athletes will know exactly what it would be like to cross the line first. They will have spent months mentally rehearsing and future pacing what they would be seeing, what they would be hearing and how they would be feeling. If we run our outcomes through all our senses we are starting to programme our minds to appreciate what success is like. If I have answered the question "What specifically will I see, hear and feel when I have achieved my aim?" then, unconsciously I will start to work towards my aim and, when I get the results, I will have clear reinforcement of my success.

Take a moment to look at your success criteria. Are they clear? Are they specific? Have you run them through all your senses?

## OWN YOUR OWN MESSAGES

If we directly or indirectly blame someone else for the messages we send, we appear weak and our overall message loses impact. So, for example, if I start a meeting by saying,

*"I think this is all a waste of time but Fred insists that we do it."*

the message my listeners receive is:

*"This person is not serious about the meeting – they are just going through the motions."*

11

It is better to take responsibility for the messages we deliver (whether we personally agree with them or not).

For example,

*"...is an important part of the current objective and I want to make sure that this meeting goes well."*

Take a look at the notes you made. Have you truly owned your message?

Sometimes people tell me they are on this workshop because they have been sent – a message that does not come across as owning. Whilst acknowledging that this may well be the case I challenge them: "You still came so what do you want to get out of this workshop? What would make it a worthwhile use of your time?"

## EXERCISE – MY OUTCOMES

Before you move on to the next chapter I would like to invite you to take a moment and think again about your outcomes in relation to presenting yourself with impact. Take a moment to revisit this exercise ensuring you are specific, use positive language and own your message.

### WHY ARE YOU READING THIS BOOK? (STATED IN THE POSITIVE)

## WHAT SPECIFICALLY DO YOU WANT TO ACHIEVE IN RELATION TO PRESENTING YOURSELF WITH IMPACT?

## HOW WILL YOU KNOW YOU HAVE BEEN SUCCESSFUL?

## WHAT WILL YOU BE SEEING, HEARING AND FEELING?

# CHAPTER TWO

# ENABLING &
# LIMITING BELIEFS

Have you ever been on a training course, or read a book, when, despite learning a lot of new skills and behaviour, you never really implemented much of the learning back in the work place? The content was all very well...but?

I recently met someone who knew all the tools and techniques of time management but who readily confessed to not putting them into practice. Her desk was a disaster zone and she argued that she never planned her day because there was no point as she would just end up having to deal with whatever was most pressing when she got into work. As a result she always reacted to situations; she knew all the principles of time management but *believed* they were a waste of time and so did not use them.

This chapter explores the impact our beliefs have on our behaviour and our overall performance. We will look at how limiting beliefs can sabotage our performance and how, by adopting more positive beliefs about ourselves as presenters, we can enhance the impression we create.

## NEUROLOGICAL LEVELS OF CHANGE

When exploring the principle of enabling and limiting beliefs I find the Neurological Levels of Change Model a helpful starting point.

The concept of logical levels of change was initially explored by Gregory Bateson, based on the work of Russell and Whitehead in mathematics. Robert Dilts then went on to apply Bateson's concept.

Logical levels refer to a fundamental hierarchy of organisation, in which each level is progressively more encompassing and has a greater psychological impact.

The levels of learning and change have been summarised by Dilts as follows:

| LOGICAL LEVEL | DESCRIPTION | KEY QUESTIONS |
|---|---|---|
| The Larger System | Vision and Purpose | Who Else? |
| Sense of Identity and Role | Mission | Who? |
| Belief and Value Systems | Permission and Motivation | Why? |
| Capabilities | Maps and Plans | How? |
| Specific Behaviours | Actions and Reactions | What? |
| Environment | External Context | Where? When? |

I have illustrated how the levels relate to one another, and some of the key questions for each level, on the following page.

## HOW THE NEUROLOGICAL LEVELS STACK UP

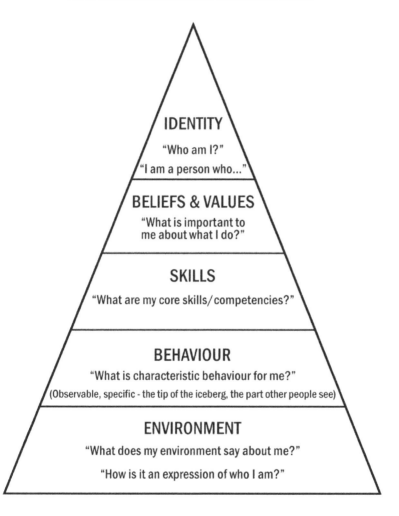

**IDENTITY**

"Who am I?"

"I am a person who..."

**BELIEFS & VALUES**

"What is important to
me about what I do?"

**SKILLS**

"What are my core skills/competencies?"

**BEHAVIOUR**

"What is characteristic behaviour for me?"

(Observable, specific - the tip of the iceberg, the part other people see)

**ENVIRONMENT**

"What does my environment say about me?"

"How is it an expression of who I am?"

The effect of each level is to organise and control the information on the level below it. Changing something on a lower level can, but would not necessarily, influence the upper levels. For example when working with teams I often hear comments such as, "It'll all be better once we're all located in the same building". They may be right, although being co-located is probably going to give rise to all kinds of conflict as a result of different behaviour, differing skill levels, different views on what the team's identity is.

In short, an environmental change is probably not going to result in many higher order changes. However, changing something on an upper level will bring about lower level changes. Using my previous illustration, if I go on a time management course and become a convert to time and self management principles, so that my beliefs change, I am more likely to adopt some new skills and behaviours back at work. My environment may also change – the desk that was once a disaster zone may become neat and tidy!

*Neurological levels separate the deed from the person. You are not your behaviour!*

Therefore, in order to bring about a change, in behaviour, skills, or environment, we need to make an intervention at the same neurological level, or one above. Bringing about a change in behaviour may need us to question some of our beliefs and values.

*"We cannot solve our problems with the same level of thinking that created them."*
ALBERT EINSTEIN

18

When talking to people about improving their presentation skills I often find that the barriers that stop them moving on and improving their skills are some of the beliefs they hold about themselves as communicators or presenters.

Often they are holding on to a lot of limiting beliefs which, until challenged and replaced by more useful beliefs, will probably continue to sabotage their performance.

Recently I was coaching Diana, a senior manager at a large multinational.

Whilst she knew she was a *very good* presenter she wanted to be an *excellent* presenter.

She felt she was very good at presenting material relating to her area of specialism and to audiences whom she felt comfortable with. However she was much less comfortable presenting to senior audiences on topics that she did not know very well – for example when she was presenting on behalf of her boss or another team member. She knew she would be increasingly called upon to do this in the future. It was clear from her language that she carried around a number of beliefs about hierarchies and people in senior positions.

During one coaching session we discussed some of the people she admired as presenters because they always appeared confident and self-assured. We called these people 'exemplars'.

These exemplars included a senior army officer who was used to briefing generals, a former colleague and female role model who was now a partner at a large management consultancy and a male colleague who, in Diana's words had a "100% natural approach" and had been trained by a non-hierarchical CEO.

At the end of the session Diana decided to embark on a modelling project, meeting up with some of these individuals and discovering from them how they did what they did. In particular she was curious about how they managed to present an aura of confidence and self assurance even when they were presenting material in which they were not considered to be an expert.

Two of the areas Diana explored with her exemplars were their beliefs about themselves as presenters and how they viewed their senior audiences. Diana summarised these and contrasted them with her own beliefs about herself and how she viewed her senior audiences. I have reproduced these beliefs in the following table:

| David | Diana |
|---|---|
| • They do not expect you to be weak in front of them. You are in your position for a reason.<br>• They will respect you if you handle them.<br>• They don't know what they don't know (85% won't know as much as you). 50% given confidently is better than 85% badly. | • They are amazing as they are in that position.<br>• They know everything and are experts in everything.<br>• They view me as young and inexperienced.<br>• I don't deserve their time. |
| **Andrea** | **Denis** |
| • Adrenalin is positive.<br>• Flushing is natural.<br>• It's lonely at the top. Treat them as humans not positions.<br>• Respect them - They have done well - but don't be deferential.<br>• You are only there because they want to hear what you have to say.<br>• You know more than they do on this topic. | • It is an honour for them to meet me!<br>• They are a person ... not a position. Connect with them as people.<br>• They don't want to be put on a pedestal – they want to be treated naturally. |

As Diana compared her beliefs about presenting to senior people with those of her exemplars she became acutely aware that her own beliefs were much more limiting.

She realised that if she presented to a board of directors believing, "I don't deserve their time", she would almost certainly be sabotaging her performance. It was unlikely that she would use all her skills and resources as a presenter to really sell her message. By contrast, borrowing Andrea's belief, "You are only there because they want to hear what you have to say" was so much more enabling and put her in a more positive space to call on all her resources as a presenter. That's the nice thing about beliefs – you can borrow them!

## BELIEFS (PRESUPPOSITIONS) OF PEOPLE WHO COMMUNICATE WITH EXCELLENCE

Neuro Linguistic Programming (NLP) has developed a number of beliefs of excellence or 'presuppositions'. The idea behind these is that whilst they may not necessarily be true, it can be useful to behave as if they are! If we do so they will shape how we act and interact with others.

I have taken a number of these 'presuppositions', adapting them slightly in some cases, and put together five *Beliefs of Excellence* for communicators and presenters.

### THE MAP IS NOT THE TERRITORY

What is a map? Probably not a question you have asked yourself very often, if at all! It is a representation of the territory as drawn by the cartographer. If I asked two people in the same room to draw a map of how to get from that building to another place a few kilometres away, the two maps would probably be quite different.

One person may have drawn a map with lots of visual symbols and diagrams. The other person may have provided street names and road numbers. The question is, which one is correct? Of course they are both correct according to the people who drew them.

Let's think about this in the context of communication. As individuals we interpret what is going on in a situation by referring to our own past experiences. We each have our own mental map of the world which we use to make decisions. However, if I step into the belief that the map is not the territory, this helps me appreciate that other people have different experiences, language and culture and that the same thing may mean something very different to someone else. Holding on to this belief means that I do not assume that my map must be a) the correct one and b) the only one which is useful in a given situation. I make the effort to understand other people's maps so that I can be sure we are on the same wavelength.

## YOU CANNOT NOT COMMUNICATE

I was talking to a prospective coaching client recently and he was recalling a meeting that had gone very badly. He told me how one of his colleagues had gone totally off message and shared information and committed to actions which had not been agreed in advance. This meeting had taken place 10 days before our conversation and, as he spoke, I could sense his anger. The muscles in his face became rigid, his eye contact became more intense and his face became flushed. As he concluded his account I asked "What did you say to him afterwards?"

He immediately retorted "Nothing, I was so angry I couldn't speak, but I hid my emotions. He has no idea how I feel, but I do need to have the conversation."

Ten days on I could sense the anger he had felt and I am sure he communicated a lot to his colleague. I refer to this involuntary communication as 'leakage'!

It is impossible *not* to communicate with people. The actual words we use only account for a small part of the overall meaning of communication. We 'leak out' so much more information via body language, tone of voice and gestures. We are constantly communicating with people – when we walk into a room, sit in a meeting, and greet people for the first time. What is our unconscious communication saying about us? Are we projecting the image that we want to project?

## THE MEANING OF THE COMMUNICATION IS THE RESPONSE YOU GET

Imagine you are delivering a presentation and it becomes apparent that some of your audience have misinterpreted what you said. You could respond in a number of ways. You could assume that you have a less than bright audience today and that this is going to be hard work for you as they are not going to pick things up very quickly! Or you could reflect that maybe you did not put that across very well as a few people seem to have misunderstood and perhaps you should try again. The difference between these two approaches? The first lays the blame for the misunderstanding on someone else. In the second you own the situation and take responsibility for putting it right.

What this belief says is, as a communicator, I know that sometimes others will misunderstand the point I am trying to make. The message I intend to send will be different from the message that is received. When this happens I take responsibility for any misunderstanding and find another way to put my message across.

## IF WHAT I'M DOING ISN'T WORKING, I CHANGE WHAT I'M DOING

The illustration I often give for this belief is the stereotypical English person abroad who does not speak the local language. What do they do? The joke is, of course, that they speak louder, in English. Amusing, but how often do we do just that with our communication? Metaphorically, we speak louder in the same language?

I gave this illustration at a workshop some time ago. One of the participants laughed, and volunteered that she was famous for sending long detailed e-mails which invariably she did not receive a response to. I asked what happened when she did not receive a response and she immediately replied "I just send the same e-mail again". Not surprisingly, this strategy generally did not work!

How often is this true for us? Receiving no reply we send another e-mail. It might be better if we pick up the phone and call the person, or go and see them in person. The challenge of this belief is that, if we are not getting the results we want, we should face up to why that might be so and have the flexibility to try a different strategy, to change our input to the system and get a different response.

It may not be the response we want but we can keep trying different strategies until we are successful.

## THE PERSON WITH THE MOST FLEXIBILITY IN THEIR THINKING AND BEHAVIOUR HAS THE BEST CHANCE OF SUCCEEDING

If I set out for a round of golf with just a putter do you think I'll be able to get round the course? When faced with this question most people concede that I would – although it would not be a very elegant round of golf and would probably take me a long time! But how about if I set out with a range of woods, irons and a putter? At this point everyone agrees that I would be much better placed to play a decent round of golf. There are some powerful parallels between this example and communication skills. If we do something really well but that thing does not work in every context our ability to influence others is severely hampered. People who are good at influencing others generally have a lot of flexibility in their style.

At this point I am often challenged, "What about X?" (Invariably a very senior person in their organisation). "X only has one way of working and that seems to be effective."

That may well be true. If we are a very senior person we probably have a lot of position power, people will do things because we tell them to, and we may not have to rely on having to adjust our style to suit others. But I do not think it is quite as simple as this. Time and again I have had senior people come to me for coaching because things had changed in their organisation and their old ways of working were no longer effective.

I vividly remember someone I coached a number of years ago. He had been with the same organisation for 22 years, since leaving university. He had a very definite way of working, saw most things as either black or white and had worked in this way all his life. He was now Director of a large region of the organisation and had recently acquired a new boss. His new boss had been a colleague for many years and had a totally different way of working. My coachee's style of working did not work with his new boss who saw everything in shades of grey. My coachee was lost and felt powerless. His new boss was frustrated with him and suggested coaching.

When I first met him my coachee was very suspicious of coaching and told me that he had attended a number of training courses in the past but had always left before the end. We spent much of our time working together focusing on differences between people and trying out different ways of working. It was a very painful experience for my coachee and particularly difficult to go through at such an advanced stage in his career. Ultimately it turned out to be a very successful coaching assignment, enabling him to adopt a more flexible approach.

At its simplest this belief says that, if I have flexibility in my thinking and behaviour I have choices available to me. If one choice does not work I can try another until I succeed.

## INSTALLING NEW BELIEFS

The good news is that we can experiment. We can try on a belief and notice how this affects our behaviour and actions. We all have the capability to:

- Recognise that we need to change our current thinking
- Identify any unhelpful or limiting beliefs from our past that we carry around with us
- Explore more helpful or enabling beliefs
- Adjust our beliefs to be more in line with the beliefs of excellence
- Use the beliefs of excellence and other enabling beliefs in our future interactions

One quick and easy way of installing new beliefs is to use the 'future pacing' technique, referred to in the previous chapter.

Future pacing involves imagining doing something really well at some point in the future. It is a form of mental rehearsal. Substantial research in the sporting world has shown that mentally rehearsing an activity is almost as effective as physically doing it. In the same way as this tool can be used to improve sporting performance, it can be used to prepare for presentations and meetings and change beliefs. Have a go at the following exercise.

## EXERCISE – INSTALLING NEW BELIEFS

Identify a past situation when you would have liked to have presented yourself more effectively and created a better impact.

Ask yourself, "What were the limiting beliefs that got in the way of me getting the results that I would have liked to get?" (For example did you believe that you were too inexperienced for your audience; did you think that your way was the only way of doing this and got thrown off course when challenged by a member of your audience?)

Consider how your current limiting belief could be modified or changed. What would it be helpful to believe instead?

Decide to start to use this new belief and let go of the old one.

Mentally rehearse putting your new enabling belief into practice. In your mind journey back to a time just before the incident happened. This time take with you i) your new belief and ii) a feeling of confidence that you can do better than before. Use the new belief to change what is happening. Notice the difference it makes to act in accordance with this new belief. Run through the incident, making changes to what is happening as many times as you need to in order to get a sense of having completely absorbed the belief into your way of thinking. This is how different it can be from now on.

Quickly check that the new belief is a good one for you. Does it fit with your value system and who you are?

Now imagine using this belief in some appropriate future situation. Run the belief through all your senses – visualise what you would be seeing, hear what you would be hearing and feel what you would be feeling. Move forward with this new belief. Practise making decisions based on this new enabling belief and reward yourself every time you do so.

By adopting this process it is possible to take on board and reinforce more positive enabling ways of thinking and, in doing so, enhance and develop your communication and presentation skills.

## EXERCISE – LOGICAL LEVELS OF CHANGE

This is one of my favourite exercises and I use it a lot on workshops and with coaching clients. It is easier if you can get a colleague to coach you through it and ask you the questions but you can coach yourself, with a little self discipline.

Create five cards with one logical level on each – Environment, Behaviour, Skills, Beliefs and Values, Identity. Start by standing where you can take five steps forward. Lay the logical levels cards on the floor in front of you in the above order, each one a step away from the last.

Imagine that it is three months from now.

- You have been working on presenting yourself with impact.
- Your hard work has paid off and you have noticed some great results.
- Better still others have noticed too!

Really associate with that sense of you as a great presenter, notice what you are seeing, hearing and feeling.

Starting at Environment, work your way up the logical levels as described on the following page, starting from the bottom of the page.

## Step forward into IDENTITY

- How would you describe yourself as a presenter?
- Express this as a metaphor. What symbol or image comes to mind that seems to express your identity as a presenter?
- Take a small step forward and truly associate with this image of you as a presenter.
- Savour this moment. Notice how you are standing, your posture, your feelings and emotions.

## Step forward into BELIEFS & VALUES

- What is important to you?
- What enabling beliefs do you have about you as a presenter?

## Step forward into SKILLS

- What skills are you using to Present Yourself with Impact?
- What skills are you particularly noticing yourself drawing upon?

## Step forward into BEHAVIOUR

- What are you doing?
- How would you describe your movements, actions and thoughts?
- What are others observing you doing?

## Step forward into ENVIRONMENT

- Where are you? Where are you demonstrating your newly acquired skills?
- Describe your surroundings. Who is around you?
- What do you notice particularly about your Environment?

## START HERE

30

Take this image of you as a presenter and turn around so
you are facing the direction you have just come from.

## step forward into BELIEFS & VALUES

- Take the physiology of the Identity level with you.
- What is important to you now?
- What do you believe now?
- What beliefs and values underpin your identity?
- Capture this new sense of your beliefs and values

## Step forward into SKILLS

- How are your skills enhanced?
- Are there any additional skills that you are using?

## Step forward into BEHAVIOUR

- What do you notice about your behaviour now?
- What are you doing more or less of?
- What are other people noticing?

## Step forward into ENVIRONMENT

- What do you notice now about your Environment?

**Take a moment to notice what is different now you
have brought all of these levels of yourself to it.**

I am often asked why the exercise takes you up through the logical levels and then back down again. The reasoning behind this is that there is a layering effect as you go through the exercise.

I find people generally find it easier to describe their environment or behaviour than they do to describe their identity. It is not a question that we tend to ask ourselves every day! Therefore going up the levels in this way is usually easier for people.

Once you have described your identity and truly stepped into it, it is amazing how you start to notice new beliefs, skills or behaviour as you go back through the levels. Usually the changes people notice are about new beliefs/skills/behaviour/details of their environment that have now come into focus. Also, if you step into a new, enabling belief as you work your way up the logical levels you will definitely notice some changes in the lower order levels as you work your way back down. It is an incredibly powerful exercise and a great way of experiencing logical levels in action.

# CHAPTER THREE

# BUILDING RAPPORT

## WHAT IS RAPPORT?

If we want to sell our message and get our audience onside as quickly as possible, it is vital we create a positive connection or affinity with them. This is rapport. Although rapport is a word used quite frequently I find that most people have never thought about what it really means. During a workshop, I often pose the following questions to get people thinking:

What is rapport and how do you know you have it?

If you were observing two people having a conversation how would you know if they had a good rapport? What might you be seeing and hearing?

Most participants will answer the first question as a sense of feeling comfortable with someone, having a connection, feeling at ease, sharing the same values, a sense of both coming from the same place.

The second question tends to provoke some interesting discussion. At first participants will provide general comments: "they will be chatting together and look comfortable", "they will be nodding", "they will look interested in each other", "they will both be laughing".

As the discussion develops people will get more specific about what they will be seeing and hearing. "They will be making lots of eye contact", "their body language will be similar", "they will be matching and mirroring each other", "they will be using similar words/expressions or finishing off each other's sentences".

Someone may even comment that the two people may in fact be saying very little but you just know by looking at them that they are very comfortable in each other's presence. They do not need to talk to fill the silence.

As we continue to discuss rapport, participants will often talk about individuals they have known for years and how, when they meet up, it is as if they have never been apart. They are immediately on the same wavelength again. Conversely others may recall how they met someone and they just clicked straight away – "it was as if I'd known them all my life!"

I see some interesting examples of this instant rapport during workshops.

I start by asking participants to provide some kind of introduction to themselves. A favourite activity involves choosing pictures from our extensive library of photographs which say something about them/their personality. As the exercise progresses I notice that people will start to refer to other people's presentations: "It really resonated with me what Julie said about ...", "I nearly chose that photograph for exactly the same reason!" "Well I also like to travel and I've chosen these photographs because ..."

When debriefing the exercise participants often volunteer how they felt a connection with someone because of something they said or did. Interestingly, when I ask people to choose a partner for the next exercise, individuals who have found an immediate connection gravitate towards each other.

# BUILDING RAPPORT

As we explored in the previous section, if you are observing two people who are getting on very well together you will notice that their body movements match or mirror one another.

As one person leans forward the other will follow. If one person crosses their legs the other soon does likewise. Where rapport exists, this happens quite naturally and spontaneously. It is also true, however, that if we consciously adopt the same sort of body postures as the other person (without obviously mimicking them) then we can build rapport and increase the receptivity of the other person without relying on a chance meeting of minds. The same is also true of voice quality and even breathing. If we start our conversation by matching the volume and pace of a person's voice then this builds a powerful sense of rapport at an unconscious level. There are four methods of gaining rapport:

## MATCHING BODY POSTURES

The most obvious method, this entails subtly matching body postures, gestures and hand movements to support/emphasise communication.

## MATCHING VOICE TONE OR TEMPO

Matching the other person's voice tone or tempo is a good way to establish rapport in the business world and an excellent method over the telephone when you are unable to see the other person. Tones can be soft or loud, high or low, fast-paced or slow-paced. Matching does not need to be exact – just close enough for the other person to feel understood.

## MATCHING KEY WORDS/PHRASES

Using the exact words or phrases spoken by the other person, and even supporting these with matching gestures, will establish a sense of connectedness and rapport with the other person.

## MATCHING BREATHING

Another method of establishing rapport, particularly effective when you cannot see the other person, is to match breathing rates. Once you have detected the other person's rhythm you can pace yourself into it. This is not as hard as it sounds as you can simply breathe out when the other person pauses in conversation and breathe in when they are speaking.

In all the above methods, once we have matched a person (match) and established rapport (pace) we can then change our voice or body language and the other person will follow us, i e we can lead. Leading is important because, if we change a person's external manner, we also alter their emotional or mental state. By first matching a person's posture and gestures and then changing our gestures to be (say) more open and relaxed we could help to turn a more reserved and quiet colleague who is unwilling to contribute fully to one who will share some of their thoughts and observations.

When discussing the above Match-Pace-Lead rapport building model in a workshop I often give the following example:

*"Imagine that at lunchtime I invite you all to go for a walk with me. We meet at the bottom of the stairs and I immediately set off walking very fast at 6.5 km an hour. What would happen?"*

Occasionally someone says that they would be up for the challenge and they would go along with me and maybe even try and walk faster! However, most people freely admit that they would let me get on with it – they would either go at their own pace or give up but they would not follow me at my pace.

I then ask "What would happen if as we set off I matched the general pace of the group at, say 5 km per hour (match) and walked at this pace for sometime ensuring that everyone was comfortably walking along with me (pace) and then gradually started to walk faster, say picking up the tempo to 5.5 or 6 km per hour?" (lead).

The vast majority of people immediately volunteer that they would happily walk along with me and not even notice that I had picked up the tempo. If they did they would probably only notice at the end when we stopped walking.

This, for me, is how true rapport building works. All too often rapport is seen as a quick "did you have a good journey here today?" before I turn to my business and attempt to lead you somewhere else. Building true rapport is about me taking time to make a connection, explore your world and match how you communicate (voice speed, volume, tone, expressions used, posture, gestures) before attempting to lead you elsewhere, maybe looking at a different way of doing something, presenting a new approach.

# THE TRUE MEANING OF COMMUNICATION

If you pick up a book on body language, chances are the book will refer to studies carried out by Albert Mehrabian in the mid to late 1960s on body language and non-verbal communication.

Mehrabian concluded that, when communicating feelings and attitudes, only 7% of meaning is directly taken from the words that are spoken. Mehrabian referred to 38% of meaning as being 'paralinguistic' (the way that the words are said including tone, volume, rhythm, speed, pitch and clarity) and 55% of meaning as deriving from facial expression (eye contact, skin colour change, expressions).

Although this 7/38/55 ratio is widely presented as a communication truth, many have questioned how far the results from Mehrabian's study can be generalised. That said, I believe the essence of the model is powerful and helpful. The model certainly reminds us that it is dangerous to place undue reliance on words alone for conveying (sending and receiving) communication, especially those which carry potentially emotional implications.

We have all had the experience of listening and watching a politician speaking on television. The words are perfect, well-rehearsed and you cannot fault them. And yet, somehow you just do not believe them. Something about the voice tone or speed or the non verbal expressions does not quite match up. In such situations we tend to believe the *signals* that we are picking up, rather than the *words*.

These additional non-verbal and verbal signals are often referred to as the "meta message". Meta is Greek for beyond. So, listening at the meta-level means listening beyond the words. Skilled communicators have the ability to listen at the meta-level. They carefully check the non-verbal response against the verbal one to see whether they contradict or complement each other. This helps in developing assumptions, forming questions and confirming viewpoints. Skilled communicators also listen to how well the words they hear match with the tone of voice that they are said with.

Equally, of course, the other party reads your body language to determine their attitude to you. It follows then that if you control your meta message so that it harmonises with your words, you will increase the effectiveness of your communication.

## BUILDING RAPPORT IN WRITTEN COMMUNICATION

In recent years e-mail has become one of, if not the, major form of communication in business. Whilst it has many advantages, it is not without its drawbacks. There is no non-verbal communication; it is almost impossible to pick up additional meaning through tone (apart from, perhaps *shouting* or *laughing out loud*). We are therefore left with just the words and often these are abbreviated or grammatically incorrect (the same norms of grammar, spelling and punctuation used for letter writing are often not applied to e-mail).

I am frequently asked how you can build rapport with someone if your primary means of communication is e-mail. It is more difficult, but there are definitely things you can do. Consider the following e-mail exchange.

Tom

Just to confirm our meeting next Tuesday at 4 pm.

Fred

Dear Fred

Many thanks for your e-mail. Good to hear from you! Hope you had a lovely holiday and have returned to work feeling really refreshed. Look forward to hearing all about it! Janet will be coming along with me. I think you've met Janet before? (She worked on the Wright account with me).

Anyway, she's really looking forward to working with you on this account. See you next Tues!

Warm regards
Tom

I have exaggerated the styles somewhat to make a point. There is an obvious mismatch between the two styles. Fred's style is direct, to the point, no small talk, whereas Tom's is much more chatty and informal. Assuming that Tom wants to make an impact on Fred – perhaps Fred is a client – there is a danger that Tom's style may be perceived as too chatty for Fred. If Tom wanted to match Fred's style he could send a more Fred-like response. For example:

Fred

Great. See you then.

Tom

Short, to the point, and more in keeping with Fred's style.

Aspects to bear in mind when seeking to build rapport via e-mail are:

- Form of address (For example Tom: Tom, Hi Tom, Dear Tom)
- Form of sign-off (For example Warm regards, Kind regards, Cheers, Regards)
- Degree of chattiness and informality
- Length of e-mail – short and to the point, longer more detail
- Matching of key words and phrases used by the other person
- Matching of sensory preferences – visual, auditory, kinaesthetic (See Chapter 4)

## EXERCISE – BUILDING RAPPORT VIA E-MAIL

Think of someone that you would like to have more impact with and a greater level of rapport and who you have communicated with in the past via e-mail. Look back over some of your e-mail exchanges. What do you notice? How much does your style match the style of the other person? In what ways does your style mismatch theirs? What could you do to match their style more closely? What will you do differently the next time you send this person an e-mail?

## BUILDING RAPPORT WITH A LARGE GROUP

The previous techniques are highly effective for building rapport one-to-one or with a small group but you may be wondering how rapport can be built with a big audience, for example, if presenting to a large group? The following are suggestions, some of which are discussed in later chapters.

## MAKE AND MAINTAIN EYE CONTACT

It may not be possible to make eye contact with all your audience individually but they should feel as if you have spoken directly to their part of the audience. Think about

41

making eye contact even before you have said a word so you can make the earliest possible connection and maintain it with all areas throughout your presentation. (See the **Walk on** exercise in Chapter 7). In a workshop it is always a measure that a person has done this when someone says "I felt as if you were speaking directly to me" and several people chorus, "So did I!"

## CONSIDER YOUR AUDIENCE

As we have already discussed, rapport is all about connecting with someone so, in order to build a connection, it is useful to think about your audience.

- Who are they?
- How knowledgeable will they be?
- What is their general attitude likely to be?

You can then use the Match-Pace-Lead model to take the audience from, for example, their current level of knowledge about something to a deeper level or a different perspective.

## USING HUMOUR

Humour can be an extremely effective way of building rapport. An audience will laugh together at a joke from a comedian on stage. This sense of doing something together is a great way of building rapport. The audience has a shared experience and the comedian has started to develop a connection with his/her audience. Offensive or inappropriate humour can also, of course, destroy rapport so it needs to be used carefully. Consider including a joke, a shared story or getting your audience to do something together at the start of your presentation.

# EXERCISES - BUILDING RAPPORT

Our ability to listen, to let go of our own agenda and focus 100% on someone else's words, message and unspoken words is a key skill for building rapport. If we can pick up on what is important to someone we can skilfully package our own ideas so they dovetail. Try the following levels of listening with a partner to gain an appreciation of what it like to actively listen and develop your skill.

## LISTENING AT LEVEL 1, CHATTING WITH RAPPORT

Decide who will be the speaker and who will be the listener.

The speaker's role is to talk about a recent experience e g a holiday, hobby, project at work.

The listener's role is to:

- Listen to the words and interpret the story in terms of your *own* experience.

- Make frequent comments offering your own opinion and sharing your own experiences.

- Think about how you would have done it differently or how you might improve on what your colleague did.

After five minutes or so share what it was like to listen at Level 1 and to be listened to. What was going on for each of you at the time? After a short debrief change roles.

## LISTENING AT LEVEL 2, CURIOUS LISTENING

The speaker's role is to talk about the same story.

The listener's role is to:

- Get into rapport with your partner (matching and mirroring body language, matching posture, maintaining eye contact, matching tone/volume/speed).

- Ask questions to clarify and seek more information.

- Summarise/reflect back/paraphrase.

- Be curious. Show by your body language that you are interested in them and their story.

- Be alert for your partner's values as they are expressed in the story – what is important to your partner?

- Stay completely focussed on your partner by listening and responding at Level 2. Do not add any opinions or views of your own.

After five minutes or so share what it was like to listen at Level 2 and to be listened to. What was going on for each of you at the time? How was the experience different from listening at Level 1? After a short debrief change roles.

# FOOD FOR THOUGHT

### 1 – WHO DO YOU HAVE RAPPORT WITH?

Think of a friend or colleague with whom you believe you have great rapport. This will probably be someone with whom you have a good, easy-going relationship, someone you feel comfortable talking with, whose company you enjoy. As you think about them, ask yourself:

- What does it feel like to be with them?
- How do I feel when I'm talking to them?
- What similarities are there between me and this person?

### 2 – WHO WOULD YOU LIKE TO HAVE MORE RAPPORT WITH?

Think of someone with whom you do not currently have a good level of rapport. This could be someone you work with or an acquaintance. As you think about them, ask yourself:

- What does it feel like to be with them?
- How do I feel when I'm talking to them?
- What differences are there between me and this person?
- What could I do to match this person more closely – be it via body language, matching tonality/ pace/volume or language? Remember we like people who are like us so what can you do to be more like them?

### 3 – CHANGE YOUR MEANING, NOT YOUR WORDS

Repeat the phrase "OK, I'll do it", three times, altering the tone of your voice each time. Focus on sounding:

- Bored and slightly irritated.
- Trying to hide your excitement.

- Resigned and compliant.

Notice how the meaning or intention of the phrase changes each time your voice quality changes.

## 4 – GO WATCH SOME RAPPORT!

Go anywhere where there are couples or groups of people – a pub, cafe, airport lounge. Spend some time watching people talk and interact. Notice the 'dance' between them, how they match and mirror each other, how they stand or position themselves in relation to each other. Ask yourself the following questions:

- How do I know whether people are enjoying each other's company or not by watching them?
- Can I tell whether people are old friends or strangers? If so how?
- What seems to be affecting the way people move or behave?

# CHAPTER FOUR

# ENGAGING ALL THE SENSES

When preparing a presentation I have noticed that most people tend to spend a lot of time preparing the **what** of their presentation. This is the rational part, including the content and the order in which it will be covered. All too often the **what** is thought through, immediately converted into PowerPoint slides, and the presentation is ready!

By contrast, the **how** is usually ignored. How can the information be conveyed so that it appeals to the broadest possible audience? This chapter will explore some of the different ways we take in and process information. We will spend some time thinking about using language, audio visual aids and even ourselves as props, to engage all our audience.

First let us think about what happens in the communication process.

This process begins with our **perceptions**. We store images through our eyes, hear sounds and words through our ears and smell through our noses. Our feelings are formed from outside information (things we can touch and feel) and from our internal emotions.

Of course we do all the above some of the time but we also all have our own set of preferences. We all have our own unique window that we use more than others. But how can we identify these preferences and use this information to understand others more and communicate with a wide audience, all of whom have their own unique set of preferences?

By now you are probably wondering what your preferences are. How do you use your five senses to process information? If you would like to answer this question before moving on take some time to do the **Your Five Senses Exercise** below.

## EXERCISE – YOUR FIVE SENSES

This exercise works best in a group, with one person reading out the instructions, and the others making some notes on their own. At the end of the exercise participants share their experience of the exercise. The exercise can also be done on your own. Just work through the questions making notes and then follow the directions to reflect on your answers. Alternatively ask a friend to read out the instructions for you.

I am going to give you some specific instructions so that you use one of your senses at a time. I am going to ask you to make a mental note of the first thing you do as I give you my instructions. I will ask you what you made of my instructions.

Before we start take a moment and examine your five senses. What can you see as you sit here now? Notice the sights around you. Do you notice anything new? What can you hear around you? Are there any sounds that you can hear now that you were not aware of before? Now be aware of what you can feel. What new feelings are you suddenly conscious of? These may be emotional or physical. What tastes or smells do you notice?

I am now going to take you through the five senses one at a time. Ready?

1. The first thing I would like you to do is to SEE AN ELEPHANT. What just happened? What is the first thing you did as I gave you that instruction? What kind of elephant is it? Where is it? Which way is it facing? Does it have a size or shape? Is there anything else about that elephant? Are you using any other sense beside sight to experience seeing an elephant?

Write down a brief description of how you just saw that elephant.

2. Next sense. I would like you to LISTEN TO THE SOUND OF A TELEPHONE. What just happened? What is the first thing you did when I gave you that instruction? Can you hear it? What kind of sound is it? Where is it? Does it have a shape or size? Are you using any other sense besides hearing to listen to the sound of a telephone?

Write down a brief description of how you made sense of my instruction.

3.  Next sense. I would like you to SMELL COFFEE. What just happened? What is the first thing you did when I gave you that instruction? Can you smell it? What kind of coffee is it? Does it have a shape or size? Where is it? Are you using any other sense beside smell to experience smelling coffee?

Write down a brief description of how you made sense of that instruction.

4.  Next sense. I would like you to TASTE LEMON. What just happened? What is the first thing you did when I gave you that instruction? Can you taste it? What kind of lemon is it? Where is that lemon? Does that lemon have a shape or size? Are you using any other sense to support you in tasting lemon?

Write down a brief description of how you made sense of the instruction to taste lemon.

5.  Next sense. I would like you to FEEL CASHMERE. What is the first thing you did when I gave you that instruction? Can you feel it? Does that cashmere have a shape or size? What kind of cashmere is it? Whereabouts are you feeling it? Is there anything else about that cashmere? Are you using any other sense beside touch to experience feeling cashmere?

Write down a brief description of how you made sense of the instruction to feel cashmere.

6.  Now notice if there are any senses that you were able to use more fluently than others. Are there any senses that occurred more frequently in that exercise e g do you repeatedly get a feeling for things even when not instructed to? Do you repeatedly make a picture of something? Note down any patterns that you notice in yourself.

Now I would like to give you a word to make sense of and this time you can use any sense you like. I would like you to notice the order in which you use your senses. The word is PETROL. What just happened? Did you see it, feel it, hear it? Does it have a size or shape? What happened next? Write down a brief description of how you experienced the word PETROL.

The next word is TRUST. What just happened? How did you make sense of the word trust? Which senses did you use? Whereabouts is trust? Does it have a size or shape? Write down a brief description of how you experienced the word TRUST.

Notice any patterns in the way that you made sense of the words PETROL and TRUST and how they relate to the answers you gave to the earlier questions. Notice your predominant senses. Now, if working in a group, compare your answers and experiences of this exercise.

Typically what emerges from this exercise is that most of us have clear preferences regarding which of our senses we use. It is very common for someone to report that they saw strong visual images throughout, even when instructed to do something else. For example you may have visualised a telephone when instructed to listen to the sound of a telephone, seen a lemon when asked to taste one, seen a black cashmere jumper when asked to feel cashmere. Equally you may have felt a strong feeling when asked to listen to the sound of a telephone, for example a sense of someone close to you calling, and you may have experienced strong reactions to some of the words including petrol and trust. In working with individuals I find that the visual and feelings preferences are the most common but it is not unusual to meet someone who makes little use of visualisation.

I recently used this exercise during a workshop. All the participants worked in the finance department of a large organisation. They completed the exercise on their own and I then invited them to get into small groups and share their responses and experience of the exercise. As they organised themselves into groups I overheard one of the participants say to his colleagues, "Well my learning is that you only need sight. I visualised everything!"

I then observed his facial expression as one of his colleagues commented that he had not visualised any of the words. He had not seen the elephant but he had heard its footsteps softly padding through the jungle and stepping on twigs and had experienced a strong sense of the elephant's presence.

Another colleague commented that he had experienced strong feelings and emotions in relation to most of the words and that these had typically presented themselves ahead of any other senses. As we shared the experiences in plenary some commented that they had not been able to taste anything, others that they had struggled with the sense of smell.

To wrap up, I asked the participants to share their learning. Interestingly the participant who had visualised everything stated that his biggest learning had been around how different people are. He had expected that, as all the participants worked in finance and had similar jobs, personality-wise they would all be very similar. He suddenly realised that his one size fits all way of presenting did not work for everyone.

"All very interesting", you may be saying, "But how can I pick up on other people's preferences and use this knowledge to better understand and communicate with others?"

Essentially there are three ways of picking up clues – via eye accessing cues, use of language and vocabulary and physiology (gestures and breathing).

## VISUAL
People who have a preference for visualisation see the world in pictures and recalled images. When communicating they use visual imagery for example, "I see what you mean", "I get the picture". People with a strong visual preference will typically support their words with hand gestures, usually at shoulder level or above and will breathe from their upper chest, often speaking quickly, as if the words are literally spilling out of the visual images they have created. Further clues are available by watching eye movements; people with a

preference for visualisation tend to either look upwards, as if they are literally visualising images and pictures, or forward in an unfocused manner. It's as if the image they are looking at is literally between you and them.

## AUDITORY

People who favour the auditory window have a preference for sounds and words. The spoken word is very important to them and they may like music, the radio, poetry and the theatre. In contrast to people with a visual preference, people who are very auditory breathe more deeply in their chest. Their speech is often slow and melodic. Further clues are available in their eye movements. When recalling sounds people with an auditory preference usually look towards their ears, that is, their eyes will move to one side or another, moving on a level plane. Sometimes people with an auditory preference will literally lean one ear towards you as if in an effort to hear all the words you are speaking. Their speech patterns are populated by phrases such as "That rings a bell", "That sounds good" and "I hear you".

## KINAESTHETIC (FEELINGS)

People who have a kinaesthetic preference represent thoughts as feelings which may be internal emotion or the thought of a physical touch. We can include taste and smell in this category of feelings. People with a kinaesthetic preference breathe lower down in their stomach than those with visual or auditory preferences. Their speech is slower and punctuated by pauses, giving them time to reflect. They will often look down and to the right whilst having a conversation, while possibly maintaining their own inner dialogue. Gestures are generally downwards and used to emphasise emotions. For example they may say "I had a really warm feeling" and as they do so put their hand on their stomach, indicating the part of the body where they experienced that feeling. Further evidence is available in their choice of language, often using such phrases as "That feels right to me" and "That made an impact on me".

You will probably find that you have a preference for one system over the others, both in the way you think and in the way you communicate.

Examples of ways that attendees at a meeting might imagine a successful outcome could be:

| | |
|---|---|
| **Visual** | An image of all the actions written up on flipcharts with names and timescales against each one |
| | An image of yourself and/or others at the end of the meeting looking satisfied |
| **Auditory** | People talking at the end of the meeting and making comments such as "That was a really useful session" and "I know exactly where we're going now" |
| **Kinaesthetic** | A sense of achievement and satisfaction |
| | A warm feeling inside, the meeting was worthwhile and productive |

By identifying and matching the unique windows of others we can more easily establish rapport and, most importantly, communicate with them using language they easily understand and respond to. For example if the person you are communicating with is using predominantly visual language and you respond using expressions like "Yes, I see what you mean", "I get the picture", "Looks good to me" or "I can't quite see that point", you have much more chance of getting into rapport with them quickly and effectively. You may well find that those people who put you at ease immediately are operating in your favourite system.

By contrast if you use predominantly auditory language e g "I hear what you're saying", "sounds good to me" there is an obvious mismatch and it will be more difficult to strike up easy rapport.

A number of years ago I was asked if I was interested in coaching a Director at a very large public sector organisation. I, and another three coaches, were asked to meet him so that he could choose the person who seemed to be the best fit. Although I was keen to do the work, I was slightly concerned about how long it would take me to travel to the client's place of work and wondered whether telephone coaching would be an option.

When we met, he immediately enquired, "Shall I paint a picture of the situation for you?" He then gave me the background to his request for coaching. As he spoke I noticed that he constantly looked up and away from me and used incredibly visual and descriptive expressions. At the end of his summary he turned to me and said, "Have I put enough colour on the picture for you?"

I realised that telephone coaching would probably not be a preference for him and decided to offer him some options.

"Well", I said, "There are various ways in which we can work together, one of which is face to face..." "Oh yes," he said, "It'd have to be face to face, I'd have to see you."

And that was that! I got the work and we never did any telephone coaching!

# EYE ACCESSING CUES

As mentioned above we can pick up clues as to individual sensory preferences by observing where people look when they are conversing with us. Broadly speaking people tend to look up when they are using visual images, either remembering a specific event or constructing an image. Alternatively they make look straight ahead, maybe even appearing to be looking at us but in an unfocused manner. It is as if they have constructed a screen between us and them and are seeing images on this screen.

By contrast, when people are accessing pure sounds they tend to look towards their ears - their eyes will move from side to side but this time on a level plane. Again, as demonstrated in the following figure, they will tend to look to **their left** for remembered sounds and **their right** for constructed sounds.

They may also look downwards. Again, broadly speaking people will look down and to **their right** if they are accessing pure feelings and emotions. Looking down and to **their left** is an indication that an individual is accessing their own internal dialogue, maybe talking something through inside their head.

As a word of caution the above eye accessing cues have become a very popular aspect of NLP and it can be very easy to see one piece of evidence and immediately jump to the conclusion that this person is very visual or auditory. The direction of glance can be different depending on whether someone is right or left handed. Many years ago I ran a workshop which included some work with eye accessing cues. We were getting some unusual results and I then discovered that, out of the 12 participants, 11 of them were left handed! It was a very useful lesson in the importance of calibration! It is important to remember that although eye accessing cues can be a useful indication of preferences, they are only one aspect to take into consideration - along with language, gestures and voice quality.

## WHAT THE EYES CAN TELL US

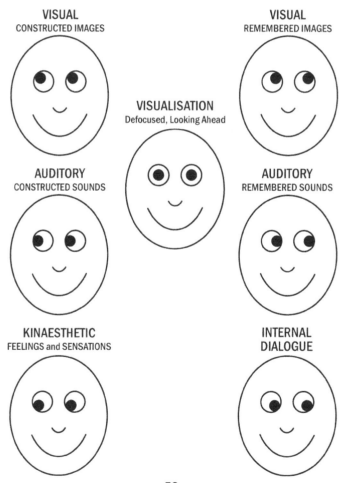

VISUAL
CONSTRUCTED IMAGES

VISUAL
REMEMBERED IMAGES

VISUALISATION
Defocused, Looking Ahead

AUDITORY
CONSTRUCTED SOUNDS

AUDITORY
REMEMBERED SOUNDS

KINAESTHETIC
FEELINGS and SENSATIONS

INTERNAL
DIALOGUE

# DIFFERENT LANGUAGE PATTERNS

The following table displays a number of words from each of the representational systems - visual, auditory and kinaesthetic. Take a moment to read through them. Which ones form part of your regular day to day conversation? Which ones can you not imagine yourself using? Are there any additional visual, auditory or kinaesthetic words that you use on a regular basis?

| VISUAL | AUDITORY | KINAESTHETIC |
|---|---|---|
| Picture | Tune | Touch |
| Clear | Tell | Taste |
| Focus | Note | Feel |
| Perspective | Accent | Smell |
| See | Ring | Sense |
| Flash | Shout | Handle |
| Bright | Growl | Throw |
| Outlook | Tone | Finger |
| Spectacle | Sing | Shock |
| Glimpse | Sound | Stir |
| Preview | Hear | Strike |
| Short-sighted | Clear | Impress |
| Look | Say | Move |
| Distinguish | Scream | Impact |
| Illustrate | Click | Stroke |
| Hazy | Static | Tap |
| Paint | Rattle | Rub |
| Cloud | Ask | Crash |
| Clarify | Chord | Smash |
| Graphic | Amplify | Sharpen |
| Colour | Harmonise | Tangible |
| Show | Key | Crawl |
| Reveal | Volume | Irritate |
| Expose | Voice | Tickle |
| Depict | Compose | Sore |
| Screen | Alarm | Grab |
| Look | Screech | Relaxed |

Some of the key expressions for each of the three systems are:

**Visual**
That looks good to me
I see what you mean
I take a dim view of that
That's clear
Can you show me how that works?
Can you illustrate that for me?
You're painting a very colourful picture of that
The future looks brighter
I look forward to seeing you

**Auditory**
I hear what you say
Sounds good to me
That strikes a chord
That rings a bell
He's out of tune with the rest of the organisation
I am glad to hear it
Tell me how it is
Listen to yourself
I am pleased you said that
It was music to my ears

**Kinaesthetic**
That feels right
That's really grabbed my attention
Get in touch with reality
Warm regards
I have got a grasp of what you mean
Hold on
I sense that something's not quite right

## SPEAKING TO APPEAL TO ALL THE SENSES

By now you probably have an idea of what some of your own preferences are and which senses you use more fluently than others. Useful knowledge, as we prefer to communicate with others as we would like them to communicate with us. Those with a strong visual preference, for instance, will be likely to present a message using visual language supported by visual props: flipcharts, pictures, PowerPoint slides. This will work well for others with strong visual preferences. However, someone who is strongly auditory may find this style difficult to follow and frustrating. They will prefer the spoken word and the opportunity to have a discussion.

Some time ago I ran a presentation skills workshop where all of the participants had to bring along a prepared presentation which they then delivered and received feedback on at the workshop. One of the participants was a very elegant woman with a rich speaking voice, full of variety and depth. During her introduction she told us that she sang in a band and liked amateur dramatics.

Her presentation, *The Rhythm of a Course*, was very different to the others. She set out to explain the lifecycle of a course in her faculty of the university. She had one flipchart which she brought to life with rich auditory language and, as she spoke, she beat time on the flipchart stand.

At the end of the presentation the rest of the participants commented on how skilfully she had used the auditory sense. They commented on her use of language, the title, the beating out of the rhythm.

However, they also commented that they would have liked some additional material to look at.

The participant was flabbergasted. She was oblivious to the beating of time and commented that she would never normally have used any visual aids as this was not a preference for her. She did not need to see things. However, she had made a concerted effort and prepared a flipchart for her presentation. She believed her presentation had predominantly used the visual sense. Yet, despite her efforts, her preferences had clearly revealed themselves!

Consider the following descriptions of the same concert, each from a different perspective.

1. *What a vision! An entire symphony orchestra, resplendent in their black and white formal attire. The conductor, majestic on his podium, sweeping the air with his arms, baton in hand. As the violinists' bows moved backward in synchronised unison I sat transfixed watching the spectacle unfurl before me.*

2. *What a sound! The melodious tones of the solitary oboe, the soft accompaniment of the violins, and the gentle beat of the drum. Gradually the noise swelled to a crescendo. Crash! The symbols sounded, the after-shock reverberating throughout the hall. Then silence.*

3. *What an experience! The full gamut of emotions! A gut wrenching melody brought tears to my eyes and a lump to my throat. Then suddenly the mood changed - sadness giving way to joy, seriousness to frivolity. My heart lightened and I felt myself relax. I settled into my chair and smiled.*

Which description did you prefer and which gave you the richest experience of the concert? Now have a go yourself at the following exercise.

## EXERCISE - ENGAGING ALL THE SENSES

Rewrite the following story using only language from your least-preferred representational system.

*The weather is bad. There is a man on a bicycle in the distance. It is difficult to cycle and he has a problem staying on his bike. He stops for a rest. The temperature changes and the cyclist resumes his journey. A lorry comes by. The lorry driver makes a noise to announce his presence and the cyclist falls off his bike onto the wet ground.*

### MY VERSION OF THE STORY:

How easy was it to just use one of your senses and switch off all the others? How easy was it to use your non-preferred representational system?

I am often asked how these ideas are used in real life and for some actual examples.

My favourite illustration is to show a slide saying:

> *I was thinking earlier, wouldn't it be nice if everyone could just get along together instead of having all these divides. Maybe a few of us could get together and make a stand. What do you think?*

I ask people what impact the words have on them. Most express a fairly neutral perspective, some say it was a bit "wishy washy" but generally OK. I then ask who else repeated a very similar sentiment, albeit much more eloquently and memorably. Someone will always twig that my speech is a very poor paraphrase of Martin Luther King's *I have a dream* speech. I then show another slide with the following extract from the speech:

> *I have a dream today!*
>
> *I have a dream that one day every valley shall be exalted and every hill and mountain shall be made low, the rough places will be made plain, and the crooked places will be made straight. This is our hope, and this is the faith that I go back to the South with.*
>
> *With this faith, we will be able to hew out of the mountain of despair a stone of hope. With this faith, we will be able to transform the jangling discords of our nation into a beautiful symphony of brotherhood. With this faith, we will be able to work together, to pray together, to struggle together, to go to jail together, to stand up for freedom together, knowing that we will be free one day.*
>
> *And this will be the day when all of God's children will be able to sing with new meaning.*

I ask participants what impact this speech has on them. It always has a powerful impact, even though the religious overtones and rhetoric may not be to everyone's taste. Somebody will point out the visual language with another person immediately referencing the kinaesthetic language. The auditory language – *jangling discords* and *symphony of brotherhood* – always gets a special mention!

Try going back to the Engaging all the Senses exercise and rewrite the story this time using a balance of visual, auditory and kinaesthetic language – without making your story three times as long!

Of course engaging all the senses goes further than just using a mix of visual, auditory and kinaesthetic language. Here are some thoughts about how you can address each of the senses when giving a presentation.

**Visual**
- Using diagrams and pictures on PowerPoint slides, flipchart or white board (A picture paints a thousand words)
- Using visual language to illustrate your message with words
- Taking care to make the environment look attractive and inviting
- Using your body to bring your presentation to life e g via gestures, facial expression, being animated
- Using visual props
- Asking participants to visualise situations/experiences

**Auditory**
- Allowing time to explain your ideas, invite discussion and questions
- Using auditory language
- Paying attention to your voice - particularly if you tend to speak in a monotone. Add variety to your pitch, tone, volume and pace to keep your audience interested
- Paying attention to sounds e g having music in the background as people arrive

**Kinaesthetic**
- Encouraging hands-on if it is a demonstration
- Passing round relevant objects, giving your audience something to touch and hold
- Appealing to the audience's emotions by using kinaesthetic language
- Making the environment appealing – is the room comfortable, not too hot or too cold, are the chairs comfortable, is the seating appropriate, are you ready to receive visitors when they arrive?

---

## FOOD FOR THOUGHT

Your introduction is your chance to make an impact. Think about writing and rehearsing a great opener which engages all the senses.

For example:

*"It's great to see so many people here today and recognise a lot of familiar faces. I was talking to a number of you over coffee and you told me how excited you are to be here and how you are very much looking forward to hearing everyone's ideas and agreeing a clear way forward."*

# CHAPTER FIVE

# LANGUAGE OF INFLUENCE

The previous chapter explored how we can use language to enrich our message by engaging all the senses. This chapter continues the theme of how the words we use can impact on the message received. How our language can influence in a positive way, as well as how we can limit our influence by using less powerful or negative language. We will also explore some of the patterns of language which, if used skilfully, can positively influence our audience.

## INFLUENTIAL LANGUAGE PATTERNS

When I introduce these patterns in a workshop I occasionally meet with the following concern – "Isn't this straying into the territory of manipulation rather than influence?" It is a very good question. Whre is the boundary between influence and manipulation? I would suggest that the difference is all around the intention behind what I am trying to do. If I am genuinely looking for a win-win situation, as opposed to trying to 'sell' you something that you really do not want, then that is more about influence than manipulation. In addition, I point out that the language patterns I am introducing are ones that we are already using in everyday life. The difference is I am putting them into the participants' conscious awareness so they now have choices about how they use them. They can continue to use language patterns in an arbitrary and unconscious manner or they can start to consciously use language patterns to enhance their message.

As you analyse the following language patterns you will notice that many of them are artfully vague, encouraging the listener to find their own level of meaning to which they will have higher commitment. Some of them have a hypnotic quality to them and it will not surprise you that a number of them are used in hypnosis. The patterns are useful at getting the listener into a positive way of thinking. You will notice that the unconscious answer to a number of them is affirmative.

For each pattern I have provided a couple of examples and gone on to explain what the language pattern is doing. I have then left room for you to write your own example, one that you could imagine using yourself. When you come to use these in a presentation I would suggest that you use them sparingly and with skill. Overuse them and you will sound far too rehearsed and inauthentic!

## MIND READING

Examples:

- *"You are probably asking yourself what you can do about this."*

- *"You might be thinking what your outcome might be."*

When describing a mind read I often use the analogy of planting a seed in someone's head. It is a very deliberate seed and directly linked to the thought that I want them to have. In the first example you are now focussing your attention on "what you can do about this".

Why? Because I suggested you do just that!

In the second example I have deliberately planted the seed of "thinking what your outcome might be". My audience is now concentrating on exactly what I want them to be concentrating on. I want them to think about that rather than what happened in their last meeting or preparing for their next one.

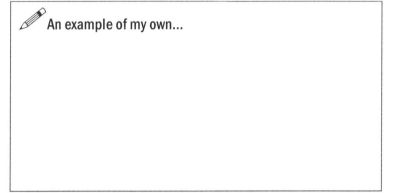

An example of my own...

## PACING

Examples:

- *"So we've heard Gill's presentation, listened to Tracy's views and discussed the main implications and we're now going to turn to next steps ..."*

- *"So we've covered outcome based communication, the importance of engaging all the senses and we are now going to move on and have a go."*

In Chapter Three we looked at the Match-Pace-Lead model for building rapport. Pacing is a technique which can be used to take the audience from where they are in their thinking (match) to where you would like them to be (lead). Pacing can be used in a variety of contexts: to link points or activities; to set out what you are going to cover; to link subjects different speakers have covered at a conference.

---

✎ **An example of my own...**

---

## CONVINCER PATTERNS - THE POWER OF THREE

Research around convincer patterns has shown that, on average, people need to have heard something and mentally agreed with it on three occasions prior to being in a **yes** way of thinking. Although, of course, some people will never be entirely convinced and others will need very little convincing. Pacers therefore often have three components.

One of the best examples I have come across of a Pacer and Convincer Pattern at work is Earl Spencer's Obituary to Diana, Princess of Wales on September 9, 1997.

*"I stand before you today, the representative of a family in grief, in a country in mourning, before a world in shock."*

You will notice that in just one sentence the context shifts from a family's grief to a country in mourning to a world in shock. Having established the scene of a world in shock Earl Spencer then delivered his own powerful message, one which I am sure those of us who heard it still vividly remember today.

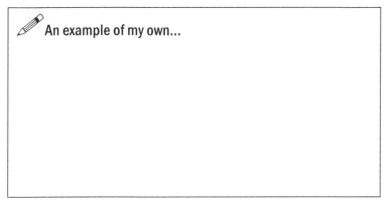

## IMAGINE YOURSELF (EXPERIENCING BENEFIT)
Examples:

- *"Imagine yourself waking up each morning and looking out at this beautiful view"*

- *"Imagine yourself being recognised as the person that solved this problem"*

- *"Imagine yourself getting people to want to do what you want them to do"*

As you will have noticed "imagine yourself" works by inviting people to create their own experience. You give them a context but stop short of providing any concrete details of this experience. Your audience is free to step into creating what that experience would be like – for them. "Imagine yourself" can work well when you want people to experience right now what it will be like in the future. It can be particularly powerful where there might be a time lag and some pain to go through before that benefit can be experienced. For example:

*"Imagine yourself in six months time presenting yourself with huge impact!"*

---

✏️ **An example of my own...**

---

## PRESUPPOSITIONS

Examples:

- *"You can do this even better"*

- *"You are learning many things"*

- *"You might wonder who is going to volunteer for this project"*

- *"You may have wondered how else you can use this in your day to day work"*

As you read the above examples you will notice that each one of them has at least one presupposition buried in the sentence. For example, the first example assumes that you can do this in the first place and that it can be done even better. The third example presupposes that someone is going to volunteer for this project! You will also notice that all of the presuppositions are positive and enabling. As mentioned in the introduction to this chapter, be mindful that any presuppositions you use are used with integrity and in win-win situations. For example, the hard sales technique, "Do you want it today or tomorrow?" may not fit with the above criteria for you.

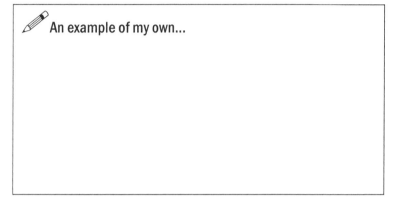

**An example of my own...**

## TAG QUESTIONS

Examples:

- *"Isn't it?" (It's enjoyable to learn something new – isn't it?)*

- *"Can't you?" (You can do that – can't you?)*

- *"Won't you?" (You will do that – won't you?)*

As you'll see from the above examples, tag questions are two-word questions tagged on the end of a sentence, to which the answer is "yes". If used with skill they can be very useful at getting an audience into a "yes" and positive way of thinking.

For example:

> *"So you saw how easy that was. You could do that – couldn't you?"*

Well yes, of course you could!

---

🖊 **An example of my own...**

---

## EMBEDDED COMMANDS

Examples:

- *"You can begin **to relax**"*

- *"I have been wondering how you might begin to **see a way forward**"*

- *"I know you will begin to **feel motivated**"*

An embedded command is precisely that, a command or suggestion that is buried in a sentence. In the above examples the embedded commands have been highlighted.

Each command is suggesting the action that the speaker wants you to take, for example **relax**. As a word of caution, be aware that embedded commands also work in the negative. For example "**Don't look** at my hands shaking", "**Don't focus** your attention on my squeaky voice!"

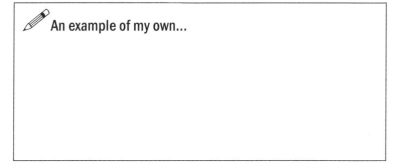

## QUOTATIONS

Examples:

- *"My colleague, Fred, once had a delegate on one of his courses who told him this story..."*

- *"My old boss used to say that anyone can ride a bike"*

- *"My friend, Philip, believes that anyone can become a great presenter"*

- *"Gandhi famously said, 'Be the Change you Want to Be'"*

This pattern offers a suggestion or idea coming from someone else. The pattern has a key advantage – you can offer up the idea but do not have to take responsibility for the suggestion.

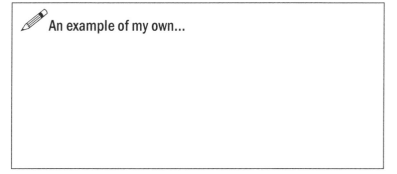

# METAPHORS/STORIES/PARABLES

Metaphors, stories and parables serve a number of purposes. At one level they engage an audience, hold their attention and are often remembered long after the presentation. At another level stories are a powerful way of accessing unconscious resources – for example linking a parallel story line or hidden meaning to the audience's own dilemma or situation.

An Example:

I vividly remember a story I was told whilst attending a Total Quality Leadership (TQL) programme almost 20 years ago. At the time I worked for a Canadian company and everyone in the organisation was attending the programme. The programme was being used as a major catalyst for change. Right at the start the facilitator told this story:

'Last summer I went camping with a friend. We went to the Rockies to do some walking. One day, out walking, we came across a bear on the path in front of us. It was looking at us in a menacing way. I was terrified. However, my friend remained very calm. He took some training shoes out of his rucksack, put them on his feet instead of his walking boots and then smiled at me. I said to him, "Are you mad? It's a bear, you can't outrun a bear". He smiled at me again and said, "Oh, I don't need to outrun the bear, I only need to outrun you!"'

It is a popular story and one you may have already heard. It served to immediately emphasise the importance of this TQL programme and the context.

Business was tough at the time and we needed to be getting new products to market quicker than our competitors. We needed to outrun them.

Of course he could have said as much, but the story and the way he told it was so much more impactful. And of course I remember it, and often quote it, almost 20 years later!

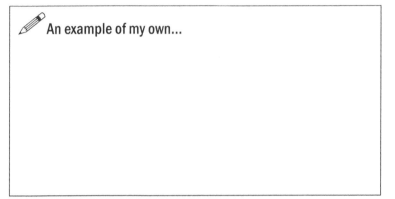

**An example of my own...**

## POSITIVE/ENABLING LANGUAGE
To Try or to Succeed?

I always feel myself inwardly groan when someone stands up to present and says "I am going to try to..."

For me it seems to reflect a lack of commitment and self confidence. The message I receive is, they may be lucky and I might get the overview they said they would try to give me. However, luck may not be on their side, they may fail in their quest and I am going to be left disappointed. Consider the following two sentences:

1. *"I am going to try to give you an overview of the new customer contact database."*

2. *"I am going to give you an overview of the new customer contact database."*

Which of the two sentences has the greatest positive impact on you?

The second sounds so much more positive, doesn't it? When coaching individuals in presentation skills I always suggest they leave out the try. Your audience will judge whether or not you have been successful in giving them the overview. You do not need to put the fact that you might not be successful in their thinking at the start!

## AND VERSUS BUT

Use "and" rather than "but".

Consider the impact of the following statement,

*"That was a great idea but I think we should do it in red and blue."*

What message do you actually hear? Most likely that it was not a great idea and the colours red and blue would be better! When we use *but* in this context it has the effect of negating whatever precedes it. Some people suggest using *however*. For me *however* is just *but* in disguise. At an unconscious level we will hear it and know that someone is actually disagreeing with us. If we use *and* instead we hear something different.

*"That was a great idea and we could do it in red and blue."*

I might still be disagreeing with you and red and blue might not work with your idea. Chances are though you will hear me out and stay with me as you have not heard a but.

## CAN VERSUS CAN'T

Talk about what you can instead of what you can't do. Can't sounds final and immediately puts an obstacle in place. Try "haven't yet" instead. It leaves the door open.

## REMOVE FILLER WORDS

People who communicate with impact use clear, positive language. They say what they want, rather than what they do not want. They also use few filler words. By that I mean they get straight to the point and do not have any obvious expressions or words, for example "you know", "okay", that they overuse. To become aware of your own filler words or frequently used expressions ask a friend or colleague to observe you in action and give you some feedback. Better still record yourself delivering a presentation and play it back. Notice expressions you use a lot and if you are using filler words rather than getting to the point. Make a note of some of the expressions you are using. How could you rephrase them to have more impact? What expressions do you need to use less often or leave out?

## EXERCISE – LANGUAGE OF INFLUENCE/LANGUAGE THAT HOLDS YOU BACK

This exercise will help you discover some of your own language patterns. I use it a lot with coaching clients; it really clarifies how you use language to positively influence yourself and others. It also focuses on how you use language that holds you back and limits your influence. It will show you how you use language patterns in all sorts of communication, written and otherwise.

## PART 1

Write down a description of a goal or vision that you are committed to and towards which you feel you are making good progress. Write down what the goal is and your progress to date and what is helping and hindering the process. Write a paragraph (several sentences) so you have a detailed description of your goal/vision.

Write another description of something that you would like to achieve but towards which you are making less headway. Write down what the goal or vision is and what is helping or hindering the process. Again write a paragraph so you have a detailed description of your goal/vision.

## PART 2

You are now going to spend some time analysing the language you use. I suggest you take two pens of a different colour, one representing language of INFLUENCE and one representing language which HOLDS YOU BACK.

Using your *language which holds you back* pen look for and circle or underline in both paragraphs:

- Words such as can't, must, should, ought to, have to, impossible.

- Generalisations such as always, never, every time (e g "I never seem to find the time").

- Expressions where the noun is missing or has become fuzzy – for example people, the situation, the institution, the company, certain things.

- Expressions which suggest procrastination – for example "When I have bought some new trainers I will be able to start jogging".

- Expressions where "I" and a sense of ownership has been removed. It is as if this goal/vision belongs to someone else.

- Woolly rather than tangible reference points – for example more sales (how many more?), improved communication (improved in what way and by how much?)

Using your *language of influence* pen circle or underline in both paragraphs:

- Words such as can, want to, really want, believe, am doing.

- Use of the word "I" and expressions which indicate clear ownership of the goal/vision.

- Any use of metaphors or analogies linked to making progress e g moving along, on a roll, whizzing along, making headway.

- Words reflecting progress that has been made – more, better, achieving, moving forward.

- Words which reflect urgency and a commitment to do it right now.

- Some sense as to how you will measure success, for example a numerical measurement or percentage improvement.

Compare the balance between the different types of language. Are you using more of one than the other? Are they evenly balanced? What conclusions can you draw about the language you are choosing and the impact this is having on yourself? On others?

Take a second look at some of the expressions you have identified as language that is holding you back. Rewrite these expressions making them positive. Speak them out loud, with conviction. How does this feel?

What parallels can you see in how you use language patterns in writing and in your verbal presentation?

# CHAPTER SIX

# CREATING A RESOURCEFUL STATE

## EMOTIONAL STATE AND PERFORMANCE

Think about the last time you watched a major sporting occasion on TV, or participated in a sport yourself, or had to carry out some high profile, difficult or exciting task.

What physical signs do you notice in people (or yourself?) before or during such an activity which tell you how they are feeling. What is their emotional state? What signs indicate good or bad performance? Does it vary from person to person?

Top performers manage their emotions so as to be at their best under pressure.

They do this by using **anchors**.

"But I'm interested improving my presentation skills, not my sporting prowess", you may be saying. "How is this relevant to me?"

Well, I believe there are a lot of similarities between high performance on the sporting field and high performance in business. Time and time again participants introduce themselves at a workshop saying that they may have prepared a fantastic presentation, know exactly what they are going to do and then, somehow, their nerves take over, their mouth goes dry, their legs start to shake and it is a case of "Here we go again...!"

For many people being able to manage their emotions and access a resourceful state (an emotional state which is useful *at that moment*, for example, confidence), is what makes a real difference to their presentation. Creating a resourceful anchor which you can access whenever you need it is an incredibly useful tool.

## WHAT ARE ANCHORS?

An **anchor** is any stimulus that evokes a consistent response pattern in a person. Sometimes these anchors are invisible to onlookers. However, others might be consistently used at certain points and become obvious. One such example would be Johnny Wilkinson's distinctive penalty kicking technique which came to the fore during the 2003 Rugby World Cup. You probably recall the steps to one side, the kinaesthetic hand hold reminiscent of preparing to swing a golf club and the eye movement indicating visualisation of the ball's trajectory.

Every time Wilkinson stepped up to take a penalty he performed exactly the same routine. Equally, the New Zealand Hakka takes the form of a team anchor, psyching up the New Zealand Rugby Team and striking fear in the opposing team. Can you think of any other sporting anchors?

As I write this chapter the 2009 World Championships have just taken place in Rome. One of the British swimmers, Gemma Spofforth, had just missed out on a medal in the 100m backstroke final the previous year in Beijing. She had been bitterly disappointed with her performance and this spurred her on to do better in

Rome. Her hard work paid off and she won the gold medal and broke the world record. A few days later she was interviewed in the Times. The article described how she prepared herself emotionally and physically for her big race.

*She rehearsed well for the moment when she walked out for her final in a state of serenity, founded on hard work and routine.*

*"I knew I'd put the hours in. It was about getting it right on the day", she says, before explaining how she managed to maintain a hawk-like focus.*

*"I always do exactly the same warm-up of 1,200m and I don't stop swimming throughout. If someone gets in my way I pull on their leg and swim over them. It's like, No! Just let me keep swimming."*

*Music is also a must. "I have two bands on my iPod: Fatboy Slim and the Prodigy. The music reminds me of the great swims I've had. It reminds me how happy I felt when things went well. It pumps me up."*

*Once the starter says "set", a deeper emotion fuels Spofforth's fire. "Virtually every race is pretty much dedicated to mum," she says. (Spofforth's mother died of cancer in 2007). "Her dedication to swimming was almost bigger than mine," she adds.*

Anchoring is generally thought to have its origins in the Russian scientist, Ivan Pavlov's work on conditioned reflexes. Whilst working to unveil the secrets of the digestive system, Pavlov also studied what signals triggered related phenomena, such as the secretion of saliva. When a dog encounters food, saliva starts to pour from the salivary glands located in the back of its oral cavity. This saliva is needed to make the food easier to swallow. Pavlov experimented, striking a bell when the dogs were fed. Over time, as the bell was sounded in close association with their meal, the dogs learnt to associate the sound of the bell with food. After a while, at the mere sound of the bell, they responded by drooling. Pavlov had anchored the sound of the bell with feeding.

We use anchors by triggering any experience using any sense that gives us the desired response.

When preparing to serve under pressure, you might get yourself into the zone by...

- *"Visualising the perfect throw, hitting the ball right in the centre of the racket and serving a clean ace!"*

- *"Hearing that sweet thud as the centre of the racket makes perfect contact with the tennis ball!"*

- *"Feeling a perfect relaxed and smooth swing and follow through!"*

It does not matter what the trigger is, as long as it works for you.

We create anchors quite naturally, throughout our lives. For example, I have an anchor associated with my full name, Gillian Margaret. Whenever I hear my full name it immediately takes me back to childhood – I'm in trouble and mum knows about it. Probably not the most resourceful anchor for me at times!

You already have many anchors that work for you. Take a moment to think about your own anchors.

# EXERCISE – MY ANCHORS

Make a note of the associations you have with the following:

- An aroma – freshly ground coffee, cinnamon, a special fragrance
- A favourite item of clothing – wearing it will give you a sense of confidence
- A specific touch
- A favourite piece of music or song
- The taste of a favourite item of food
- The view of a special place
- The memory of a moment in time
- The memory of something you did really well

Which were your most powerful anchors? Which senses were they associated with?

## PREFERRED STATES FOR ANCHORING

When thinking about setting up an anchor for yourself it is worth bearing in mind the following:

Naturally occurring states are the most intense. Therefore if I have a powerful experience of confidence, presenting fantastically, a sense of being able to walk on water, it is a great idea to anchor that state so I can access it for the future.

Vividly remembered associated specific memories from the past are less intense. For most people this will be the starting point for establishing an anchor – remembering a specific time when I was confident/energetic/ authoritative and being able to step into that memory as if it were happening again right now.

General memories of the past are even less intense. A general memory of being confident around that time is much more difficult to anchor than a specific memory.

The general memory itself will be less intense. There will be less concrete details to recall.

Imagined or constructed states are least useful. It is much better to have experienced something in the past, albeit in a totally different environment, than to imagine what something would be like.

I am often asked if the experience that is anchored needs to be related to the kind of experience we want to have in the future. For example, if I want to have an anchor of confidence when I am presenting, do I need to have a time when I have presented with confidence to anchor? The real beauty of this technique is that this is not required. Often we do not have a specific time to recall but chances are we have experienced a similar confidence in another part of our lives.

A few years ago I was working with someone who wanted to set up an anchor of confidence for herself to use when she was presenting. She told me how her nerves would take over; she could feel them starting in the pit of her stomach and, as she started to speak, they would spill over and ruin her presentation. She recognised that the sense of anticipation and butterflies in her stomach needed to be there for her to perform at her best but she did not want them to be taking over.

I asked about a time when she had that same state of confidence with a sense of anticipation and butterflies in her stomach. She immediately told me how she was captain of the company's netball team. She recounted how, before a match, she was always nervous, with butterflies in her stomach. She always acknowledged these butterflies as a good sign, meaning she was ready for the game and cared about the result. As soon as the whistle went, the nerves disappeared and the energy was channelled into her performance.

I coached her through setting up an anchor of confidence which she triggered by hearing the sound of the netball whistle in her mind. The auditory filter was very strong for her and so having an auditory anchor worked well. Through her anchor my client found a way of welcoming her nerves and butterflies – they were required for excellent performance – and of keeping them at a level where they remained productive.

By now you have had some time to think about your own anchors and I am sure you are ready to create an anchor that you can use for presenting yourself. The technique described in the next exercise is based on *The Circle of Excellence* formulated by John Grinder and Judith DeLozier. If you can, ask someone to read out the instructions to you so can concentrate on doing the exercise. However, you can do the exercise on your own also. Just read the instructions a few times until you get the idea of the exercise then have a go.

## EXERCISE – CREATING AN ANCHOR

Choose a resourceful state you would like to be able to access in the future (for example, confidence).

Identify a specific time when you fully experienced that same state of confidence.

Imagine a circle or some other shape on the ground in front of you, or select a specific colour symbol or other visual cue that you would associate with that state.

When you are ready, step forward into your circle (or symbol/shape you have chosen). Relive the experience by associating into the state fully. Imagine you are experiencing that state right now – what are you seeing? What are you hearing? And what are you feeling? What kinds of feelings are they and where are they?

Concentrate on enhancing your experience of that state by amplifying any distinctions, for example specific colours. Use all your senses.

Step out of the circle, shake off the state, and take a moment. Out of 10 how intense was that experience? If less than eight or nine what do you need to add in (or leave out) to make it 10? Maybe some extra feelings and emotions, or something else needs to be in the picture.

Step into your circle (or symbol/shape) again. Repeat steps four and five, concentrating on reliving that experience through all your senses.

Step back and shake off the state.

Test your anchor by stepping forward into your circle (or symbol/shape) and noticing how quickly and fully you can re-access the state.

If necessary repeat steps four to seven until you achieve easy, clean access to the state.

Identify some of the situations in which you would like to have this state. Imagine you can take this anchor into each situation and future pace your experience.

In a workshop I always do a demonstration of this exercise with a volunteer in front of the group. At the end of the demonstration I invite questions about process but discourage questions about how it works and whether or not it will work for individuals. As an activity it does look a little odd and can be greeted with scepticism. However, I have lost count of the number of people who have had a go and been impressed by its effect. For many people this access to confidence, or the state they want, is the single thing that has the biggest impact on their presentation skills. It leaves them free to fine-tune other aspects of their presentation.

There will be an opportunity for you to use your anchor, and do some further work around mind and body links, in the following chapter.

Several years ago my husband, Colin, was due to give a presentation to several hundred agents and distributors at a conference at the Reebok Stadium in Bolton. At the time he was not working with me and was MD of an American organisation. Although a very good speaker I knew he was nervous about presenting to such a large audience.

Later that afternoon he called me as he was driving home.

"How did it go?" I asked.

"Brilliant!" was the reply. "I used anchoring."

I was rather taken aback as I didn't know that he had taken so much interest in my work and knew about anchoring, let alone how to do it.

"Fantastic," I replied. "How did you do that?"

'I remembered the speech I gave at your sister's wedding. (The previous year my elder sister had got married and, as our father had died many years earlier, she had asked Colin to give her away. A tall order as many of the guests knew my father and Colin was stepping into some very big shoes.) As I stepped up to the podium today I saw this sea of faces and remembered all the friendly ones at your sister's wedding; I remembered the sense of pride and feeling from the audience that they were all willing me to do well and I heard Steve's voice (my mum's neighbour) saying afterwards "that was a class act!" and I just delivered my presentation.'

This remains one of the best examples of anchoring that I have heard and of course Colin still uses this anchor. Only now it is double strength as he has added in the feelings of the successful presentation at the Reebok Stadium. He has also abbreviated the anchor to 'Reebok'.

# CHAPTER SEVEN

# MIND & BODY WORKSHOP

Think about a time when something did not go very well for you. Cast your mind back to that time and the feelings and emotions that you experienced. As you sit or stand now you will notice that you do not feel that good about yourself in mind and body.

Maybe you feel a bit down, your posture has slumped, your shoulders have drooped. Give yourself a shake and think about a time when something went really well for you.

Step back into that experience right now. You will notice that you feel so much better in yourself now. You feel more positive, more upright and confident-looking.

Mind and body are connected, and I am sure we have all experienced situations when we have not felt good about ourselves and this has affected our behaviour. This has, in turn, been reflected in the results or outcome. If we are not feeling our best we are not going to put as much effort and positivity into something as we are when we are feeling really upbeat, and we will typically get worse results.

Recently I was coaching someone who was going through a major reorganisation at work. She had been very happy in her previous role but knew that this would be changing. She felt very uncomfortable about the reorganisation, was angry that she was being affected when she loved her job and had done nothing wrong, and was struggling to motivate herself to be proactive and market herself internally for a new role. She told me about a recent meeting she had attended with her Director and how badly this had gone. I asked her to describe her behaviour in the meeting.

She told me how she had arrived late and had had no option but to take one of the last remaining seats, by the door and far away from her Director who was running the meeting. She mentioned how she had hardly spoken. When the time had come for her to give an overview of the project she was running she had left it to members of her team to provide an update. She made very little eye contact with the Director and other colleagues in the group. At an unconscious level she was angry and upset and had wanted others to know. On reflection she felt she had little impact on the meeting. She had even worn a beige suit and felt that she had made herself unremarkable, like her suit.

My coachee had another meeting coming up the following week and we talked about how she could make a more positive impact on the meeting and particularly her boss. She immediately volunteered that she would arrive early and get a good seat in the meeting, as close to the Director as possible.

She would give the update on her team's project and take a lead role answering questions. She mentioned how should would sit differently and demonstrated what her alert, listening and interesting posture looked like. Finally she said she would wear her favourite, brightly-coloured suit, which made her feel really confident. As she spoke she sounded and looked a different person. Needless to say this meeting went much better for her.

At times the impact we have on others may be different from what we intended. I am sure we have all used the expression "But that wasn't what I intended!" when, in our opinion, someone misinterprets something we have said.

For example, we may intend to come across as energetic, assertive and confident. However, there are many factors that may distort that intention and create a different impact. These include the words we choose, our body language and our tone of voice. If we are not aware and careful, instead of coming across as energetic, assertive and confident, we actually come across as aggressive, arrogant and out of control. The following illustration summarises.

## INTENTION VERSUS IMPACT

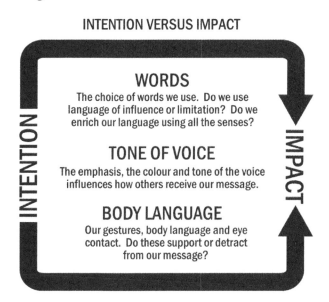

INTENTION

**WORDS**
The choice of words we use. Do we use language of influence or limitation? Do we enrich our language using all the senses?

**TONE OF VOICE**
The emphasis, the colour and tone of the voice influences how others receive our message.

**BODY LANGUAGE**
Our gestures, body language and eye contact. Do these support or detract from our message?

IMPACT

The only way we can understand the gap between intention and impact, and therefore begin to close it, is by receiving feedback and raising our self awareness. This chapter provides a series of exercises which you can either do on your own or with colleagues. They are designed to give an appreciation of body language and tone of voice when we are at our best and most impactful. Whilst you can do the exercises in any order I would recommend that you do them in the order shown. If you can record yourself on DVD so much the better!

## GETTING STARTED

Read out the words in the box below. I suggest you stand to do this.

> *I present myself with impact. I have a powerful and clear speaking voice. I support this with a strong body stance and gestures. Watch me present, listen to my words and believe my message.*

Just take a moment to reflect on how that sounded and felt to you.

We will come back to this exercise later.

## STANDING POSTURE

Most of us, especially when we are in stressful situations, tense up our bodies somewhere: possibly our shoulders, knees, neck or jaw. Stand normally in front of a mirror and concentrate on finding your point of tension. Take a good look at yourself. Where do you look tense?

Practise releasing this tension. Tense all your muscles – legs, arms, face, hands. Concentrate on squeezing really tightly and then let go. Feel that sense of release. Release any residual tension from your shoulders by lifting them up towards your ears and then relaxing them. Swing your arms around. Carefully bend from your waist, allowing all your body to relax and drop down towards the ground like a rag doll. Gently come up from the base of your spine, bringing your head up last.

Now you have relaxed your body think about creating a **firm and confident standing posture**. Lift your shoulders, roll them back and relax them down. Imagine you have a plumb-line running from the top of your head, through your spine, to the ground. The eyes should be looking straight ahead, looking *at* the world, rather than *up to* the world or *down on* the world. Your head should be comfortably balanced on a long neck.

Stand with your feet shoulder-width apart, in the same way as you would do "mountain stance" in yoga or "ready position" in a martial art, with your knees slightly soft, rather than locked. If you are working with a partner get them to push you gently on one shoulder. If you have a solid stance you will rock back gently but not lose your balance. Practise finding this good posture for yourself and standing like this so it becomes comfortable for you. Although you may move around during your presentation it is good to have a sense of your starting point and where to return to if you find you have lost your posture. This is a particularly good exercise for women to practise as the combination of nerves and high heels can lead to some very interesting and distracting postures – pirouetting, crossing feet, standing on one foot and balancing on the heel of the other! Get a sense of what it is like to be truly grounded, centred and ready for action.

Think about where you stand to present and about owning your space. I think this is particularly true for more informal and impromptu presentations where these smaller details may be lost. For example, if presenting some ideas from a flipchart, stand a little to one side rather than draped over it or hanging on to it. Be aware of presenting from a space where some of your audience cannot see you. Remove any obstacles between you and your audience.

Last year I ran a workshop in the conservatory of a hotel. At the start of the workshop the participants were asked to prepare a flipchart introducing themselves and hang it somewhere in the room. I then asked the participants to introduce themselves after which they received some feedback on the impact they had made on the group.

One of the participants placed her flipchart on one of the windows, immediately behind the flipchart stand and next to a large potted plant. I still vividly remember her presenting whilst peering out from behind part of the plant. Her reasons for attending the course were all about building up her self confidence and presence. Interestingly in her presentation she seemed to be saying, "If you can't see me maybe you won't know I'm here!"

## SEATED POSTURE

Now get a chair and sit down facing a mirror. Sit how you would do normally in a meeting and give yourself some honest feedback. How do you look? Engaged? Disengaged? Relaxed? Too relaxed? Confident? Now sit confidently, owning your own space. Keep adjusting your **posture** until you think you look both confident and comfortable. Whilst there are no hard and fast rules, crossed legs can create a barrier, particularly if you are seated directly across from someone. Crossed legs can also make it more difficult to breathe deeply from your diaphragm and make you resort to shallower chest breathing. Think about being at your best and making a real impact in a meeting. Whilst sitting back in your seat may be comfortable and show that you are listening, it is hard to make an impact from there and you need to adjust your posture and sit more upright and forward to make an effective contribution to the meeting.

## WALK ON WITH CONFIDENCE

The next exercise is a little different and works best with an audience able to give you feedback. It explores first impressions, the impact we have on a group and the rapport we build without saying anything.

Stand at the back of the room. Take a moment to ground yourself. Think about your standing posture, roll your shoulders up and back and relax them. Lift your head up (remember in Chapter Four we talked about how we look down when we access our feelings and, if we are nervous, we do not want to be gathering up those feelings as we walk on). Concentrate on making **eye contact** with your audience from the moment you come into their vision. As you walk forward imagine you are stepping into your circle of excellence and fire your anchor. Walk with measured speed and confidence to the front of the room and to the middle of your 'stage'. Make sure you arrive and finish with a strong and centred posture. Smile and make eye contact with all the members of your audience (if it is a small group) or with all sections of the audience (if it is a large group). Take a second to arrive and make contact with your audience non-verbally before you even say "good morning". If you are doing this activity with some colleagues take a moment to get some feedback on what you did well and what could have been better. If you have time have another go. It can sometimes help to have a mantra to walk on with. For example, "I am going to walk on with gravitas".

Last year I was doing this activity with a large group as part of a modular leadership programme. One of the participants who was about six foot four did his walk on to huge acclaim from his colleagues. His posture was excellent; he exuded confidence, made great eye contact and arrived centre stage looking self-assured. His feedback was, quite rightly, incredibly positive, and several of his colleagues commented that it was much easier to do this exercise and make an impact when you were so tall. It was just easier to have presence.

Fifteen minutes later it was one of his colleagues turn. This person was almost a foot shorter and yet his walk on was just as good. He walked with the same degree of self assurance and had just as much presence. He really held his space and as a result his feedback was just as good. At the end of the session the group concluded that, whilst height is a natural advantage, you can have just as much presence if you are shorter. Indeed they found that years of trying to blend in had made a number of the taller participants slouch.

# BREATHING

A common complaint I hear is "When I am nervous, I often run out of breath, my voice sounds breathy and I can hear myself breathing. I'm sure my audience can hear me breathing too!"

Good voice projection requires efficient working of the lungs, intercostal muscles and diaphragm. Think of an opera singer in full flow. He or she can sing several phrases comfortably using one breath. By contrast most people, when they are talking, take short, shallow breaths which make it difficult to maintain a constant and confident level or length of speech. This is because when we breathe we tend to hold the breath somewhere in our throat or chest rather than in our diaphragm and stomach where all the space is for air.

The diaphragm is an umbrella-shaped muscle which helps push air out of the lungs. To locate yours place your hands, with fingertips touching, across your body below your ribcage. Breathe out making the sound "huff" and you should feel the diaphragm working and see your fingertips being pushed apart.

Now practise taking a deep breath using your diaphragm. As you breathe in your stomach should expand and your fingertips be forced apart as in the previous exercise. (If you find your stomach going in, experience a tightness in your chest and your shoulders moving upwards you are probably breathing in using your upper chest.) Experiment using diaphragmatic breathing. See how long you can talk using just one deep breath.

Effective breathing has a second important benefit in that, if we are nervous, taking a big, deep breath will also slow down our heart rate and calm us down. In contrast short, shallower chest breathing will contribute to our racing pulse and nervousness. I always take a big deep breath before presenting. It helps focus my attention and gives me a real sense of being centred and ready. Practise using diaphragmatic breathing – laughter is very good exercise for the diaphragm muscle!

## VOICE PROJECTION

At times you may need to vary the volume of delivery and be able to project your voice, particularly if you are presenting in a large room. Here are two exercises focussing on **volume** and **projection**.

The first exercise looks as controlling the **volume** and **distance** of your voice. Lie on the floor and say or sing the sound of "Ho", concentrating on the sound only reaching 15 cm from your nose. Take a deep breath and hold the sound for as long as possible. Now change the distance to one metre from your nose. Again hold the sound for as long as possible. Finally project your "Ho" to reach the ceiling. What differences did you notice? How loud could you get and what did that feel like?

The second exercise concentrates on getting your **resonators** working well. Hold your nose and say "Many mighty men making much money in the moonshine" with as much force as possible. Then release your hold on your nose and say the same phrase. You will immediately hear the difference in the force of your vocal sound.

Humming before speaking is another way of improving voice projection through resonation.

## ARTICULATION

Now concentrate on removing any remaining tension from your jaw and face. Use an exaggerated chewing motion to loosen up your jaw and exercise your lips. Press your lips together, increase the tension, hold and then release. Have a big yawn, open your mouth wide and feel the back of your throat open up. Massage your face, especially around the jaw, to remove any tension.

Tongue twisters are a great way of practising articulation. Try these old favourites then start to experiment by making up your own. Start slowly, concentrating on accuracy and clarity of pronunciation then gradually increase the speed. Your target is to say them at speed and all in one breath.

*"Peter Piper picked a peck of pickled peppers.*
*Did Peter Piper pick a peck of pickled peppers?*
*If Peter Piper picked a peck of pickled peppers,*
*where's the peck of pickled peppers Peter Piper picked?"*

*"A big black bug bit a big black bear;*
*made the big black bear bleed blood"*

*"She sells sea shells by the sea shore"*

*"A tutor who tooted a flute*
*tried to tutor two tooters to toot.*
*Said the two to their tutor,*
*'Is it harder to toot*
*or to tutor two tooters to toot?'"*

*"Lesser leather never weathered wetter weather better"*

*"Red lorry yellow lorry red lorry yellow lorry"*

## TONALITY AND EMPHASIS

The meaning of our communication can change depending on where we place tonality and emphasis.

Consider the phrase: *"I didn't say he stole my bike"*

- If I emphasise *I* the meaning you receive is I didn't say it but someone else may have.

- If I emphasise *didn't* this may come across as a categorical denial – I didn't say it.

- If I emphasise *say* this may come across as me denying that I actually spoke those words, although I may have implied them.

- If I emphasise *he* the meaning you may receive could be that it was actually someone else who stole the bike.

- If I emphasise *stole* I could perhaps be implying that he borrowed it.

- If I emphasise *my* the suggestion could be that it was someone else's bike.

- And finally, if I emphasise *bike* I could be implying that he actually stole something else.

So, potentially many different meanings in one simple sentence of seven words - depending on where I put my emphasis.

Have a go with the following short sentences. How many different meanings can you create?

- *"I can't do that here"*
- *"If she could see you now"*
- *"Don't you tell me what to do"*

- *"He doesn't want to go to Spain"*
- *"I have a powerful and clear speaking voice"*

Start to experiment with nursery rhymes, famous speeches and stories. Practise on your own exaggerating the range of voice that you use.

## GESTURES

How to use gestures and what to do with our hands seem to be two very common concerns for would-be presenters. We have probably all had experience of watching people present and found our focus fixed on gestures: a pen being waved around, a hand that appears to be sewn into a pocket, too many distracting gestures, the jangling of keys or coins in a pocket. There are many books which purport to identify the rights and wrongs of body language. A popular example is that folded arms means that I am closed to you.

Personally I treat such truths with a degree of scepticism. It may just be that it is comfortable to fold my arms. Nevertheless I believe it is important to be mindful of the impact our gestures may have on others.

Where possible avoid holding on to anything which may become a distraction, for example a pen or pointer. Remove any coins or keys from your pockets and anything that might jangle and create a noise, including items of jewellery. Be aware of gestures which, when nervous, become exaggerated. For example interlocked fingers can become a white knuckle ride if tensed during a presentation. I generally advise people to start their presentation with their hands loosely by their side, allowing some air to circulate around their arm pits. Most people, as they start to present will use gestures naturally.

Consider using gestures to emphasise key points and words. Have a go at bringing the following phrases to life using as many different and exaggerated gestures as you can.

- *"The circus trapeze artists fly through the air"*
- *"The Amazon is wide, deep and broad"*
- *"His hospitality knows no bounds"*
- *"The majesty of the mountains enthralled me"*
- *"It's as big as the universe"*
- *"It's a finely honed spreadsheet"*
- *"Watch me present, listen to my words and believe my message"*

## PUTTING IT ALL TOGETHER!

Now return to the very first exercise and put everything together. Do your walk on once again and once you've arrived centre stage deliver the phrase "I present myself with impact" to your audience. Concentrate on bringing your message to life.

> *"I present myself with impact. I have a powerful and clear speaking voice. I support this with a strong body stance and gestures. Watch me present listen to my words and believe my message."*

If you do not have an audience deliver your presentation to a mirror. Take a moment to reflect on what that was like. How was it different to your first attempt? What has improved? What do you still need to work on? (You can only improve by doing these exercises. Just reading the book and thinking about it will not make much difference!)

This group of activities, which I call a *Mind and Body Workshop*, is one of my favourite sets of activities. Done as part of a workshop it is amazing the difference in participants between the first reading of "I present myself with impact" and the final delivery. Participants will comment on how colleagues appear to have grown in stature. Their delivery is less rushed due to them pausing before starting to speak. Participants add more punctuation and pauses to their delivery so their message is easier to take in and digest. In short it is amazing how much more positive an impact can be generated with a few tweaks here and there.

Doing these exercises regularly will help you develop a more confident and impactful physical presence as well as more flexibility, power and control in your voice.

# FOOD FOR THOUGHT

Several years ago I ran a development centre for a manager at one of my major clients. This work involved spending a day with a high potential individual and putting them through a range of individual and one-to-one activities after which I prepared a report identifying their strengths and areas for development. From the outset I noticed that, during the one-to-one activities, the manager communicated in a quiet voice with little variation in tone and pitch. He emitted low levels of energy and was quite difficult to listen to. As I was assessing him against the client organisation's competency framework and one of the competencies was **Communicating for Impact**, I found myself making a lot of notes about the level of impact he created during these activities.

The final exercise of the day involved working on a case study and preparing and delivering a presentation with findings and recommendations. I arrived at the appointed time and asked the manager to deliver his presentation. He immediately stood up and presented his findings and recommendations in a clear voice. For the first time he became energised and enthusiastic, his voice had so much more colour and tonality to it and he used humour to good effect. It was a complete transformation and, in my amazement, I almost forgot to make notes. I was transfixed. Was this really the same person? I could not fault his presentation.

At the end of 20 minutes I thanked him for his ideas and enquired if I could ask some questions. He agreed and sat down. Instantly his demeanour changed. He came out of presentation mode and answered all my questions in his default communication style. It was confusing and a real anticlimax.

Two weeks later I sat down with the manager and gave him my feedback. I explained the impact the two contrasting styles had on me. Interestingly it all made sense to him. He told me how he had received feedback on his lack of energy and how he tended to present his ideas in meetings in a monotone voice. However, he also knew that he was a very good presenter; he had worked on his presentation style and had received very positive feedback on this.

In his own mind giving a presentation and presenting his views at a meeting were entirely different activities. With the former he saw the need to consciously project energy, enthusiasm and modulate his voice. With the latter he had not seen any need to make adjustments. After all he was not presenting. Needless to say the rest of our discussion focussed on how he could take some of the skill and behaviour that he used in his presentation mode into his regular informal presentations in meetings and one-to-one discussions. He did very few formal presentations and was severely limiting the number of people who experienced him at his best!

## ACTION PLAN

Take some time to reflect on all of the exercises and activities you have undertaken during this Mind and Body Workshop. What actions are you going to take in order to present yourself with impact in the future?

Make some notes below...

**I will *start*, or do more of, the following:**

**I am going to *continue* doing the following:**

**I am going to consciously *do less* of the following and/or *let go* of this behaviour:**

CHAPTER EIGHT

# STEPPING INTO YOUR AUDIENCE'S SHOES

Skilled negotiators, influencers and presenters all have the ability to step into another person's shoes, to see themselves and understand how they come across to others. In other words skilled negotiators/influences/presenters are able to take different perspectives on a situation. The popular NLP activity, perceptual positions, can be an extremely effective way of appreciating different perspectives and developing your skill in this area. Consider the diagram below which illustrates three different perspectives.

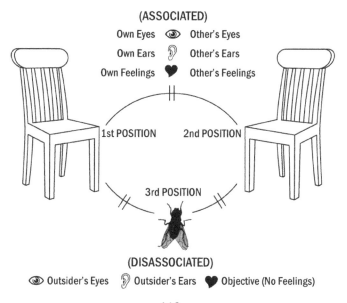

**(ASSOCIATED)**

| Own Eyes | 👁 | Other's Eyes |
| Own Ears | 👂 | Other's Ears |
| Own Feelings | ❤ | Other's Feelings |

1st POSITION          2nd POSITION

3rd POSITION

**(DISASSOCIATED)**

👁 Outsider's Eyes    👂 Outsider's Ears    ❤ Objective (No Feelings)

Sitting in the **First Position** chair I am experiencing the world through my own eyes. I am hearing sounds, the words of others or my own, through my own ears. If I truly focus on what is going on for me I can tune in to my own feelings and emotions. I can experience these as if they are happening right now. In other words I am associated with those feelings and emotions. They are happening to me.

If I now move to the **Second Position** chair I am stepping into someone else's world. I am experiencing the world through their eyes which, of course, means if I look across to my chair, the one I was just sitting in, I can now see me and how I come across to others! I can see my facial expressions and gestures. If I focus on what I can hear in this Second Position chair, I can hear my own voice – its tonality, volume, pitch. I can also get a sense of the feelings and emotions associated with someone else's world, particularly in relation to how they are responding to me.

Next I can move to the **Third Position**. This is a very different fly on the wall perspective. This involves creating some distance between the fly on the wall, and Positions One and Two. From the fly's vantage point I can observe both of us interacting with each other. I can study our facial expressions and gestures, hear our voices and notice similarities and differences between us. Crucially from this perspective I can observe how behaviour is breeding behaviour. For example the more I say or do something, the more the person I am interacting with reacts in a certain way. This perspective is different in that there are no feelings and emotions attached to it. It is disassociated, that of an impartial observer. As such, from this standpoint, I may be able to give myself some consultancy advice, based on what I am observing and hearing.

Finally, I can return to my own seat having experienced all three different perspectives. I can consider the consultancy advice offered to me in Third Position. I can also take these new insights into the future. I can imagine a future interaction with this person and how I might behave differently, and the impact that this might have on the outcome.

Gandhi is often cited as one of the most skilled negotiators and leaders of modern times. During his negotiations with the British he was frequently called upon to use all his skills. In later years he was asked how he had dealt with this time in his life, how he had prepared for what he had known would be very difficult? Gandhi invariably gave the following answer.

Firstly he would spend some time considering his own emotions and feelings. What did he believe? What did he believe to be the right and best course of action? What was important to him and to India? (First Position.)

Secondly he would step into the shoes of his opponent/adversary and strive to see the situation from their perspective. He would become his British adversary – seeing the situation through their eyes, taking on their historical and personal perspectives fully. What was important to his adversary? What did they want to have happen? At times he would enhance this perspective by actually sitting in his adversary's seat as a means of immersing himself in their world. (Second Position.)

Finally he would step outside the situation and adopt the role of the fly on the wall. From this position he would see the situation from the perspective of the outside world and ask how the rest of the world viewed this situation. What was the big picture view? What was the impartial observer's view without the emotional history of England or India?

Only when he had experienced the situation from all three perspectives would Gandhi step back into his own shoes, enriched with the insights gained from the different view points, and negotiate as the leader of India.

I believe this story illustrates how the ability to look at a situation from a number of different perspectives - our own, that of another involved person, and that of an impartial observer – can be incredibly powerful.

The real skill is the ability to shift back and forth between these positions very quickly, gaining additional insights. Imagine being able to skilfully consider your own perspective in advance, determine what is important to you and what you are thinking and feeling; then easily move into someone else's shoes and appreciate what is important to them and what they are thinking and feeling; and finally take a more detached point of view and be aware of the interactions between the two of you.

Let us think about how we can develop this mental agility by considering the following scenario.

# EXERCISE – ANOTHER PERSPECTIVE

Paul and David have started working together on a new business development project. Paul is very creative, his written work is often messy and unstructured and he pays little attention to detail. David is very thorough, tidy and works in a very structured and organised way.

- Paul sends David an e-mail saying he has attached his initial ideas on the project and asking for his input.

- David opens the attachment. The document is unstructured, mainly a series of notes which are hard to follow with a lot of spelling mistakes and grammatical errors. David spends the next hour formatting the document, correcting the spelling and grammatical errors and sends it back to Paul with a note saying "I've tidied this up for you".

- Paul opens the revised document. All he can see is David's corrections which he has done in red. His ideas have been turned into a three page report. He can barely recognise his original ideas! In addition David does not seem to have critiqued any of the ideas or added any of his own.

- Paul fires an e-mail back to David: "Thanks, if I'd wanted an English lesson I'd have asked for one!"

Imagine that David is your client. He has come to you somewhat bewildered about what has gone wrong in his interaction with Paul and seeking your advice going forward.

1. First step into David's shoes. What is he seeing, hearing and feeling? What is important to David?

2. Now put yourself in the shoes of Paul. What is Paul seeing, hearing and feeling? What is important to Paul?

3. Finally take the perspective of the fly on the wall. What is the fly seeing? Hearing? Is the fly noticing any patterns of behaviour – for example the more David does one thing the more Paul does something else? And, finally, if you could offer one piece of consultancy advice to David as your client

what would it be? Remember it needs to be something that David can do himself. Whilst it might be tempting to suggest getting a new work colleague or that Paul has a personality transplant, neither of these are within his total control! Instead think about what he can do to influence the situation.

As you considered the above scenario you may have found that you empathised more with either David or Paul. You may have found it easier to adopt some of the positions than others. I remember demonstrating this activity many years ago as part of an influencing skills workshop. As I finished the demonstration one of the participants broke the silence by stating "Yes, but it's really difficult to put yourself in someone else's shoes, isn't it?" Before I had time to say anything one of the other participants countered "No, I spend my entire life in second position!" I knew the second person very well and, from what I had observed, there was a lot of truth in his statement. He did spent a lot of his time in second position. He was extremely good at empathising with others. He would anticipate other people's needs and invariably put them above his own. As a result he was known as a great team player and colleague but tended to struggle to assert his own position. He spent very little time thinking about his own perspective ahead of an important meeting or negotiation and, as a result, did not make a strong impact on others. He also often came away with outcomes which benefited others and not himself.

Thinking specifically about the topic for this book, **presenting yourself with impact**, we can see that all three perspectives have a different part to play in the kind and level of impact that we have on others.

## FIRST POSITION

This perspective is useful when expressing your ideas and opinions, being clear about your message, pursuing self interests, taking care of yourself and your needs, making decisions and commitments. However, if we spend too much time in first position we can appear selfish and egocentric and be unaware of our impact on others.

## SECOND POSITION

As we explored in Chapter Three, this perspective is useful when establishing rapport, listening and understanding others and where they are coming from. However, as illustrated in my example above, if we spend too much time in second position we can become too acquiescent and too accommodating. We can reduce our impact by putting too much emphasis on the needs and wants of others.

## THIRD POSITION - THE FLY ON THE WALL

This perspective is useful when you encounter obstacles or strong emotions as emotions are taken out of the equation in this position. It can also be useful for taking stock, moving in a different direction or taking in the bigger picture. However, if you spend too much time in this position you can appear detached from your feelings and emotions and those of others, too rational and perhaps cold and condescending.

I vividly remember the first time I experienced perceptual positions as an exercise. I was taking part in an Introduction to NLP Workshop and had just had the exercise explained to me and watched a demonstration. I remained sceptical about the exercise and how it worked. All the participants were invited to pair up and have a go, coaching each other through the exercise. We were invited to think about a situation where we would like more understanding around the dynamics of the relationship and to have more positive influence over the individual. I decided to use a relationship with one of my clients – my best, at the time, in terms of the amount of business they gave me. However, the relationship always felt strained and I would leave a meeting fractious and irritated.

I had no problem stepping into First Position and went on at some length about the other person's annoying habits and mannerisms! Things started to get interesting as I (Gill) moved into Second Position. As the client I noticed that, when I started to question Gill's ideas or suggest my own she (Gill) became defensive. Her body language changed, her eye contact became more fixed and aggressive. In addition she started to use the expression "in my experience" a lot. Being several years younger than Gill and not as experienced in the field, I (the client) felt exposed and as if she was challenging my position. I therefore started to push my own ideas more and emphasise that I was in this case the client!

As I moved into the Third Position, the fly on the wall, I noticed a very interesting cycle of behaviour. The more the client challenged Gill's opinions, the more Gill dug her heels in, referring to her own considerable experience in this field. In turn, the more Gill referred to her experience, the more the client started to insist on what he – as the client - wanted. It was clear that neither was listening to the other. In this fly on the wall position I was invited to offer a piece of consultancy advice to Gill. I suggested that next time, instead of immediately challenging her client, Gill could listen to what he had to say. She could show an interest, ask questions, instead of immediately offering a different approach. I suggested that she needed to let the client feel important rather than belittled.

Returning to my own position I felt enlightened and immediately started to think about how I could use these insights at my meeting with the client the following week. The next day I sent him an e-mail and suggested that, as our meeting was late afternoon, we met in a less formal environment than usual, maybe over a coffee? (We tended to meet facing each other over a table in a small office with no windows. The scene was set fair for a confrontation!) He immediately suggested we met at the coffee shop across the road.

We started as we always did. I outlined a proposal for a piece of work he had requested and he immediately offered a different approach. I suppressed my desire to go into my "I'm older and more experienced" mode and instead asked questions exploring his ideas. I even managed to incorporate one or two of them into a revised overview. Somehow it felt different, less confrontational, and easier, more about us rather than me and him. When we had finished, my client commented on how he felt it was the best meeting we had ever had. And I came away with even more orders for business. Truly a win-win!

By now I expect that you want to have a go to see what insights you can gain by taking some different perspectives.

Here are some useful tips before you get started...

- Until you get very skilled at this activity create different spaces/seats for each of the positions and make sure you move spaces/seats each time you move position. (If you do not move positions there is a good chance that you will be trying to be someone else whilst still being you – which is very difficult!)

- Make sure you 'break state' after each position: clear your mind and physiology of the last position, give yourself a shake, think about something totally different (I often think about smelling freshly ground coffee). This gives you a better chance of accessing a new position unencumbered by the baggage of the previous position.

- I find it helps me get into someone else's shoes if I think about how they sit/stand and talk, and adopt their posture, mannerisms and way of speaking as much as I can.

- Finally, when you adopt the fly on the wall position, create some space between the first and second position spaces and this new position so you can be more objective. The more emotionally attached you are to your own position, the more distance you need to create between this role and the fly on the wall.

Now you are ready to have a go!

# EXERCISE – TAKING A DIFFERENT PERSPECTIVE

Think of a situation where you would have liked more influence and a greater level of impact. We can use this example to explore some different perspectives. (This exercise works best if you can remember a specific occasion). Create three separate spaces/chairs. (I often have the fly on the wall position as a standing role from where I can observe positions one and two).

Step into first position. Fully connect with being you. Imagine you are in that situation with the other person right now. What are you seeing? What are you hearing? What are you feeling? What do you want? What is important to you? Once you are sure you have fully explored this position stand up and break state.

Step into second position. Imagine being the other person on that specific occasion. Think about how they sit, speak and behave and, as much as possible, adopt the same posture and mannerisms. As this other person, what are you seeing? (Remember if you are looking through their eyes you will be seeing you). In second position what are you hearing? What are your feelings? What do you want? What is important to you? Explore this role ensuring that you keep in their shoes. Stand up and break state.

Step into the detached fly on the wall position. From this neutral stance, you are looking at you and the other person over there. You are watching and listening to them communicating – words, tone and body language. Ask yourself: what do I notice? What am I seeing and hearing? In this impartial position you have no feelings and emotions so put these to one side. Pay particular attention to any patterns you notice. For example, is there any behaviour that is breeding behaviour? Is there any behaviour from one person that causes the other to do something else? Finally you might want to think about a piece of advice that you can give to your client – which of course is you! Break state.

Step back into first position with this balanced thinking and new insight. What are you experiencing now? Think about a future interaction with this person. What can you take from this exercise and try out in future? Concentrate on your own actions rather than what other people could do to make your life easier. If you are struggling, remember the belief of excellence from Chapter Two: "If what I'm doing isn't working I change what I'm doing". Anything you do that is different to what you would normally do will change the system. You will have stopped the cycle of behaviour breeding behaviour. You will inevitably get a different response, even If this is not the one you want, and you can then start to experiment until you get your desired outcome.

Perceptual positions can be an extremely useful tool in many different situations where we want to understand and positively influence the impact we have on others. We can use them to understand and increase the impact we have on others in formal or other presentations. One of the most creative uses of perceptual positions to increase impact I have come across is described below:

I was coaching an individual who was at risk of redundancy and looking for another job. He asked me to take a look at his CV and a recent letter of application and give him some feedback. I told him that, whilst they were both factually correct, they lacked impact. In particular, he had not sold himself at all in the application letter, which did not inspire or excite me or in any way stand out. He agreed and readily admitted that he found it very difficult to "blow his own trumpet". Interestingly he volunteered that he found it very easy to sell the skills and knowledge of others.

We had explored perceptual positions in a previous coaching session and I suggested that he might find it easier to write his application letter from a different perspective, for example the fly on the wall. In essence he would be writing a letter of application in the third person, as if it were for someone else. When he was satisfied that he had created the right impact for this person he could then change the pronoun from *he* to *I*. My client readily embraced this challenge.

The next time I saw him he presented me with a letter of application in which he clearly summarised why he was ideally suited for the role in question, using positive and impactful language. It was so much better than the previous version. I asked him how he had done it.

He told me that he had sat in a seat in his office at home from where he could view his desk. He had imagined himself sitting at his desk and from the fly on the wall position he had written a summary of all Robert's skills and attributes in relation to the role in question. He had then written this up into a letter continuing to refer to himself in the third person as Robert. Only when he was really satisfied with the letter had he substituted *I* for *Robert*.

Something he had been wrestling with for several weeks had, all of a sudden, become very easy, once he had taken a different perspective.

## FOOD FOR THOUGHT

Which position did you find easiest/hardest? All three positions are equally important and one of the keys to being able consistently to present yourself with impact is to be able to move between them effortlessly. The differences you see when you look at the world from various perspectives provide a richness of information to help you adjust your style to a situation and the different people in it.

The positions you found easiest to get into are the ones you experience the world from most of the time. The ones you found hardest will be the ones that you do not use as often. They are like an underdeveloped muscle. How will you develop the positions you find more challenging?

How will this mental agility positively influence your relationships with colleagues and clients? How can you use the insights you have gained to consistently present yourself with impact?

# CHAPTER NINE

# GETTING PREPARED

It was never my intention to write a book about how to deliver a fantastic PowerPoint presentation. I wanted to concentrate on how we present ourselves in formal or informal settings, through voice and body language. Nevertheless, as I reach the end of the book, I feel it would be remiss if we did not spend some time thinking about putting all these ideas together. This chapter therefore focuses on hints and tips for preparing and delivering a formal presentation to a large audience.

## USING POWERPOINT

To PowerPoint or not? That is the question! One that hardly anyone asks, as people use PowerPoint without thinking about it. Like me, you have probably sat through many dreary PowerPoint presentations which blur into one another. So, before you start preparing your slides please consider if PowerPoint is the best medium for your presentation.

I often ask participants at a workshop, or when coaching clients, to tell me about the best presentation they have ever witnessed. Time and time again people recount stories of someone who just stood up and presented without notes, telling a story or sharing anecdotes in an engaging voice.

I do not remember a single occasion when someone has told me about a fantastic presentation delivered using PowerPoint. Often when running a workshop I invite the delegates to deliver a presentation without using PowerPoint as a crutch to remind them what is coming next. For many it is a really challenging concept.

There are some real advantages to using PowerPoint. It can be a powerful and professional visual aid. A PowerPoint presentation can also be put together quite quickly (obviously once you start to include complex graphics and sound clips your preparation time will increase) and is easy to adapt and modify for future audiences. Using a wireless remote control also enables you to move around and access other areas of the room or stage.

On the downside, too many sound and visual effects, or slides that have too much on each one can be irritating and distracting. PowerPoint slides generally show up better in a slightly darkened room but this can put people to sleep and does not encourage taking notes. You are also at the mercy of technology and you need to make sure you have all the equipment you need and that it is compatible. PowerPoint will give your presentation a formality which may work against you if you are aiming for an informal environment. Also, be careful that your slides do not become too 'busy'. An organisation I know has developed a practice of using PowerPoint slides as handouts which can be taken away and sent to people who did not attend. These are often far too detailed to be effective as presentations.

Finally, everyone uses PowerPoint. This makes it hard for you to deliver a presentation that people will remember. To have any impact you need to know your slides inside out, including what comes next. You should be using PowerPoint because it is the best medium for your topic – not just because it is easy.

# FLIPCHARTS

Flipcharts are very versatile and have some real advantages. I particularly like using them with small groups as they create an informal environment and can be used interactively - for example, you can write down responses. Completed flipcharts can also be displayed around the room as aide memoires and reference points.

They are not suitable for large audiences, however, as people who are seated any distance away will struggle to read them. Equally if your handwriting is not very clear, they can look messy, especially if you are writing whilst interacting with your audience. Over-reliance on flipcharts can also turn you into a static presenter or encourage you to develop bad habits such as leaning on the flipchart or turning your back on your audience, thereby breaking rapport.

## MY FIVE FLIPCHART TIPS

1.  If the process you are illustrating is complex, do most of the writing/drawing in advance and add only the most important details in front of your audience.

2.  Put a couple of blank sheets of paper on top of your prepared flipchart so the pages do not show through until you are ready for them.

3.  Use and experiment with colours. Red is clear from close up but very difficult to see at a distance; light colours will not show up.

4.  Use good quality watercolour pens. Permanent markers soak through the paper to the next page and permanently damage walls and clothing. If you are going to be doing regular presentations I would strongly suggest you invest in a set of quality pens. I always bring my own.

5.  Write big, and clearly enough so anyone in any part of the room can read it easily. Practise in advance.

## VIDEO CLIPS

Clips can be very powerful and enable you to use humour and/or examples from a different scenario to illustrate a point. Video also provides both a visual and auditory way of getting your information across. Your audience is provided with something different to look at and listen to. A video clip is also useful if you are going to be delivering the same presentation a number of times and want your audience to receive a consistent message.

However there is a danger that the clip can take attention away from you. Some may be too long or not relevant – after all a five minute clip gives you five minutes less to present yourself and your message! So, use clips with caution and use just enough to illustrate your point.

## PROPS

Under 'Props' I would include photographs, pictures, models, samples or anything else relating to your topic. When running workshops I encourage participants to present in a way that is different to what they would normally do. As a result many do not use PowerPoint and this has resulted in some really creative, unexpected and memorable presentations.

Props can be a good way of involving the audience, creating humour and stimulating interest. They also show that the presenter has given some time and thought to the presentation – after all that bag of props did not just materialise on its own!

You need to be careful that they do not distract your audience from what you are saying. Also, you will need more time to prepare for and set up the presentation.

## COMBINING MEDIA

Think about how to use media in the most effective way to support your presentation – sometimes a variety is the best, while at others one or two aids will do very well.

Although you may still decide that PowerPoint is the best medium for your presentation, I would still ask you to consider other media as well.

Will flipcharts, whiteboards or photographs enhance your presentation? Can you use your space so you are not presenting from a static position next to your laptop? How can you use music to create a mood or add to your message? What stories and anecdotes can you include?

One of the delegates on a recent workshop did a presentation on her time as part of a morris dancing troupe.

Her presentation included some PowerPoint slides giving the background to morris dancing and some photographs from competitions she had taken part in. An interactive piece used a flipchart, and the audience was asked to say what came to mind when she mentioned morris dancing. She used a short clip of morris dancing music and demonstrated some basic steps; she included morris dancing props (her costume, bells and scarves) draped over a flipchart stand and some anecdotes and stories made people laugh.

It was effective and memorable – as I sit here writing I can recall most of it. An excellent example of how various mediums can be combined to create a memorable presentation. It was also very obvious that the delegate had put a huge amount of time and energy into creating her presentation. PowerPoint would have been much, much quicker, but nowhere near as effective.

## STRUCTURING YOUR PRESENTATION

There are various schools of thought about how to structure a presentation, probably the most well known being: "Tell them what you are going to tell them, tell them how, tell them, tell them what you told them".

I tend to favour an approach of putting yourself in your audience's shoes (what are they thinking and asking themselves?), and then create a presentation which answers as many of these questions as possible.

### INTRODUCTION

Your introduction is a vital part of your presentation - your opportunity to make a positive impact on your audience from the start. It is also your opportunity to introduce your subject matter, and capture your audience's attention. A friend once told me that your opening remarks, i e the first three minutes of your presentation, are the only time you can pretty much guarantee that no one will interrupt you or ask questions.

Whilst I have no scientific evidence to support this view, it makes a lot of sense. During the first few minutes you have your audience's attention, they are probably interested in what you are going to say and how you will handle your subject matter, and, at this point, they are unlikely to ask any questions. Most audiences want a presenter to speak well and be interesting – after all nobody wants to listen to someone droning on! I therefore encourage people to plan and rehearse their introduction. This is the time to think about how you can use enriched language and some of the influential language patterns to really grab the attention of your audience (as explained in Chapters Four and Five). Write down the words you are going to use. Think about words that have impact and take out any filler words or ones which take away impact.

## WHO ARE YOUR AUDIENCE AND WHY SHOULD THEY LISTEN?

Having grabbed your audience's attention, and told them briefly what you are going to talk about, it is important to give them a reason for listening. One major obstacle is that human beings can think at approximately four to five times the rate that somebody is speaking. This means we tend to think about other things and not just about what is being said.

The implication for a presenter is clear – we need to hold the attention of our audience as it is very easy for them to drift off and start to think about other things. If we are not careful they will soon have lost concentration and may miss important parts of our message.

To minimise the above, think about your audience from their perspective. There will be a mixture of personalities. Some people may be happy to just listen to what you have to say. There will very likely be some who will be wondering, "What's in it for me? Why should I give up 30 minutes of my valuable time to listen to you?" I therefore advocate second positioning your audience and putting yourself in their shoes.

Some key questions I ask myself are:

- What is my audience's level of knowledge/interest in this subject right now?
- Why would my audience want to know about the topic that I am talking about?
- What is in it for them?
- Why is it important for them to know about this?
- What are the benefits for them?
- How are they likely to react to my message?
- Who are the decision makers?

I often refer to this part of the presentation as **headlining** – giving your audience a clear reason for being there and an overview as to how the presentation will go. Providing answers to the above questions in my presentation will go a long way to holding my audience's attention as I go into my topic.

## TELL THEM HOW

Next I think it is useful to provide your audience with a quick overview of how you are going to present your subject matter.

- Is your presentation all PowerPoint slides?
- Have you got a short DVD to watch?
- How long are you going to present for?
- When do you want to take questions?

Answering the above questions helps your audience know what to expect and also gives them some clear direction as to how you would like them to respond, for example in relation to questions.

## TELL THEM!

Now we come to the meat of your presentation. This is the time to deliver your prime content – any information, facts and figures, essential details, plans, timescales. Basically everything that your audience needs to know so they can make sense of what you are talking about.

## WHAT'S NEXT?

This next section depends very much on the purpose of your presentation. Some potential outcomes might be:

- **To inform** – To pass on general information to your audience.
- **To report** – To present an overall picture or detailed presentation.
- **To entertain** – To amuse your audience with stories.
- **To persuade** – To motivate your audience into action.

If your outcomes are any of the first three, a brief overview of what you want to happen next might suffice. You might want to cover how someone could use this information or what are the consequences of using it/not using it in the future.

If you want your audience to take some action as a result of your presentation you will want to spend time addressing this question. Recently I did some work with a group of volunteer fundraisers for a charity. As you can imagine this part of their presentation was crucial.

We called it, "The call to action" and here we focussed on some of the things that the audience could do, starting from that day, to get involved.

## CONCLUSION

If you have covered all the above points in some detail, there should be little need for a long conclusion. I tend to favour something punchy, a short summary of what you have covered and a recap of any steps or call to action. Recently I sat through a presentation which ended with the words:

*"I know you'd love to be part of this. Wouldn't you?"*

A great example of a mind read and tag question in action, and they combined to create the perfect ending. It was certainly hard to say "no"!

# YOUR VENUE

Where your presentation is taking place will have an impact on how you deliver it. Often the venue itself is predetermined and there may be little that you can do to influence the choice. However, there are things you can do to influence how you use the space you have been provided with; it is crucial to think about these in advance. Below are some key questions to ask yourself, and a checklist is at the end of this chapter.

## THE ROOM

First of all, how big is the room and how many people will be present?

If the room is large you will need to project your voice so everyone can hear you. Alternatively you may need to think about using a microphone. If it is a formal presentation to a large group you may even want to visit the venue in advance if this is possible.

Where will you be – on a stage or close to the audience? Being on a stage or platform is useful as all your audience will be able to see you. It may also give you more space for visual aids, props and movement.

Try to find out in advance the layout of the venue and what is going on in adjoining rooms. You do not want your presentation to be distracted by renovation work, laughter, music, applause from next door.

## THE ROOM LAYOUT

How will people be seated? If it is a large audience they will probably be seated theatre style so you will need to think about standing where as many of your audience as possible can see you and you can make eye contact with all areas of the audience – the back, middle as well as the front row.

If it is a smaller audience think about your preferred layout for you and your subject matter. Presenting to 40 people around a huge boardroom table will feel very different to presenting to 40 people seated in a U-shape with no tables.

Whilst you may not be able to adjust the seating to suit your preference, it is certainly worth asking the question in advance. In any case I would always recommend arriving early to get a feel for the room and make any last minute changes. Do not assume that because you have asked for a specific layout that you will get it. I have lost count of the number of times I have asked for a U shape of chairs, projector and screen and two free-standing flipchart stands only to turn up and find a huge board room table, pristine white table cloths and blotters and one flipchart attached to a wall!

Scan the room for distractions and obstacles - extra chairs, plants, tables. I always recommend presenting without any obstacles between you and your audience. Practise sitting in various seats in the audience. From this seat can the audience see you? Can they see the screen? Can they see the flipcharts? Are there any obstacles or distractions in the way? If there are, can you move them? Can you close curtains or blinds to minimise any distractions outside?

### FACILITIES

Finally think about what facilities you require at the venue. What audio visual props do you need and are these catered for? Is there power in the room and an extension cable? It is always better to check than to assume!

## HANDLING QUESTIONS

In the previous paragraph we explored the benefits of preparation and rehearsal, all things that we can control. But what about things that we cannot, for example, questions from our audience? How can we ensure that we present ourselves throughout our whole presentation, including the Question and Answer session, with impact? First of all it is a good idea to decide when you want to take questions and make this clear to your audience. There are benefits to taking questions as you go – it gives the audience an opportunity to have anything explained that is not clear and for you to get some involvement and dialogue. However, there is a danger that your presentation could be sabotaged, other people eat into your valuable time and that the topic goes off at a tangent.

On balance I would therefore suggest that, in most cases, it is best to take questions at the end, and that you clearly announce this at the beginning. Of course, if you do decide to take questions at the end, make sure you allow enough time. For example, if you have a 30-minute slot you may want to allow 20 minutes for your presentation and 10 minutes for questions.

## ANTICIPATE QUESTIONS

I have already spoken about the importance of "second positioning" your audience, putting yourself in their shoes. As part of this process I would suggest that you spend some time considering, having listened to your presentation, what questions your audience may have. Write these down and spend some time preparing your responses in advance. Think about the questions you would rather they did not ask, as well as the easy ones. How will you handle these difficult questions if you are asked them? Far better to have a response ready than just hold your breath and hope! If you really dedicate some time to this topic you will probably anticipate most of the questions your audience may have at this point.

## REPEAT/REPHRASE QUESTIONS

When asked a question it is good practice to repeat or rephrase the question. This practice serves a number of purposes: it ensures that everyone has heard the question, particularly important if you are presenting in a large room and someone on the front row has asked a question; it gives the questioner an opportunity to confirm that they have understood the question correctly and, finally, it buys you some time.

## ANSWERING QUESTIONS

Take your time. It is much better to take a little longer and give a considered response than rush in and give an answer that you later regret.

Make sure you understand the question and that all your audience has heard it before you even start to answer. If you need a little more time, pause, take a sip of water, remove your jacket. These pauses will invariably seem far longer to you than your audience. Although the question may have been asked by a particular individual, remember to address your answer to the general audience so that other people do not feel excluded and lose interest.

If, despite all your preparation, you find you do not know the answer to a question, stay calm. You still have some options. One is to open the question to the audience – "What do other members of the audience think?"

Alternatively, you can simply admit that you do not know. This will do more for your credibility than trying to bluff your way through. If this is your strategy tell the questioner you will find out and come back to them. If you decide to do this make sure you take their contact details, make a note of the question and get back to them after the event.

## NOBODY ASKS ANY QUESTIONS

It is fairly common for there to be a period of silence when you ask for questions. It can take a few moments for people to formulate their questions and there can be a delay whilst people wait for someone to start the process. Again, stay calm. You can even signal a pause and that you are moving into a different part of your presentation by moving to a different part of the room, removing your jacket, taking a drink of water. If no one asks a question you could anticipate a question by saying something like, "A question I am often asked is X", and then going on to answer that question. This gets the ball rolling. Finally if you do not get any questions it could be that your preparation, preparation, preparation really paid off and you have done a really through job and answered all their immediate concerns!

## DEALING WITH THE HECKLER OR DOMINATOR

Perhaps one of the biggest fears for presenters is having a heckler in your audience. Someone who interrupts, asks questions, appears to have their own agenda or tries to dominate the questioning period. My golden rule is never tackle a heckler head on. Matching aggression with aggression will only result in inflaming the situation and, worst still, you may find that some of your audience start to side with the heckler. Treat hecklers assertively, however. If you have already announced that you will be taking questions at the end of your presentation, remind them of this and ask if you can discuss their issue at the end. If it appears that the heckler is expressing a concern which is shared by others then you need to address it. Ask if other members of your audience share the same concern. If there is a groundswell of agreement, decide to address the issue there and then before you move on, or commit to addressing it at the end of your presentation and ensure that you do so.

## THERE ARE LOTS OF QUESTIONS & NOT ENOUGH TIME TO ANSWER THEM

This could be a good sign indicating that you have held the audience's attention and stimulated their interest. If you only have a limited amount of time for questions make this clear up front – "We have five minutes left so we have time for two or three questions". Take questions from different areas of the room rather than allowing one person to dominate the question time. In addition you could advise the audience that you will be available to answer any questions informally later on, for example over a coffee break and/or you could give your audience your contact details so they can contact you with any remaining questions.

## PRESENTATION LOGISTICS CHECKLIST

❑  Is the equipment working?

❑  Do you have extra bulbs, extension leads etc for projectors?

❑  Are all the audiovisual materials on hand and in the correct order?

❑  Do you have all needed supplies (pens, Post Its etc)?

❑  Is the lighting at the right level?

❑  If not, who will adjust it and how?

❑  Does the microphone work if you need one?

❑  Is the air flow and temperature right?

❑  If not, who will adjust it and how?

❑  Is there a bottle of water and glass for you?

❑  Are there enough chairs?

❑  Extras for latecomers?

❑  Are there enough handouts?

❑  Who will hand them out and when?

# CHAPTER TEN

# HAVING A GO!

## WHAT IS YOUR PREFERRED STYLE?

The fact that you have chosen to read a book on how to present yourself with more impact probably says a lot about how you like to learn. Although there are different models and theories around learning styles (for example Honey and Mumford and Kolb), all of these have a consistent theme – the concept of a learning cycle made up of four inter-related and equal stages. Honey and Mumford identify four different styles of learning which they refer to as the Activist, Reflector, Theorist and Pragmatist. I have provided a short description of each of these below.

### ACTIVIST

Broadly speaking Activists learn by doing something, by engaging in an experience. This experience can be reactive, something which happens, or proactive, an experience which is sought out. Activists tend to be flexible, open minded and happy to try out new things. They enjoy getting involved and participating with others.

### REFLECTOR

By contrast reflectors learn best by looking back at, and reflecting on, what happened. Reflectors tend to be methodical, thorough and careful. They enjoy gathering data by reading and listening.

## THEORIST

The Theorist learns by drawing conclusions. Theorists tend to be rational and analytical. They like logical structure and ask probing questions to expose flaws and inconsistent thinking.

## PRAGMATIST

Pragmatists learn by planning new experiences and applying what they have learned to what they do in the future. Pragmatists tend to be practical, down to earth and realistic. They like 'how to' hints and techniques.

Although we all do all of the above to some degree, we are likely to have some styles of learning which we prefer. For example I may enjoy doing, engaging in activities and planning new experiences based on my learning (Activist and Pragmatist) but dislike models and theories and making time to pause and review experiences (Theorist and Reflector). Alternatively I may love reading about management models and theories but find the doing, the putting theory into practice, more of a challenge. Take a moment and complete the following exercise.

# EXERCISE – HOW DO I LIKE TO LEARN?

**WHAT IS YOUR PREFERRED WAY OF LEARNING? WHICH OF THE LEARNING STYLES DO YOU PREFER?**

**WHAT IS YOUR EVIDENCE TO SUPPORT YOUR VIEWS?**

**HOW DOES YOUR LEARNING STYLE IMPACT ON HOW YOU REACT TO VARIOUS LEARNING OPPORTUNITIES (STRUCTURED, FORMAL OR UNSTRUCTURED, INFORMAL)?** Consider instances where you felt that your learning style may have facilitated or inhibited your learning.

**HOW WOULD YOU LIKE TO IMPROVE/CHANGE YOUR LEARNING STYLE?** What would you be prepared to do and how do you think others may be able to help you?

# TAKE ACTION!

Having completed the above exercise, you may have concluded that your Activist style could be stronger. If this is the case you have probably enjoyed reading all the practical hints and tips, relating the various models and theories to your own situation and reflecting on how you can have greater impact in future presentations. Chances are you have not taken much **action** yet! You may be still waiting for the perfect opportunity to present itself. You may be thinking that you need to do more reflection or preparation, that you are not quite ready yet. You may be wary of taking a risk and having a go at something you have not tried before. In which case it is time to take some action!

A couple of years ago I did some work with a coaching client. The client was at a real crossroads and focussing on a change of career which would have a big impact on her lifestyle. As we worked together I noticed that she had a very interesting pattern. At the start of each coaching session I asked her to report back on what she had done since last time. I noticed that she fed back in the form of a learning cycle. She said what she had done, how she had reflected on how this had gone, what she had concluded from the experience and how she had then planned next steps. Except that there was something slightly odd about her feedback. As I listened carefully to her words I noticed that what she was actually telling me was what she had thought about doing. She had then reflected and drawn conclusions based on an imaginary experience. Most of the time she had actually done very little.

During one of our sessions I suggested that she complete Honey and Mumford's Learning Styles Questionnaire. I was not surprised when her Activist score turned out to be extremely low and her Reflector score very high. Nevertheless this was a real insight for my client. In her mind she had confused thinking about an experience with having a concrete experience. Immediately after our session she created a sign saying *Take Action!*, laminated it and stuck it above her desk as a constant reminder that she needed to be doing things as well as thinking about them. Needless to say our coaching sessions thereafter tended to focus on what she had actually done and reflections on these experiences, rather than on actions that she had thought about taking.

If you are in danger of falling into the same trap, now is the time to put some of your learning into action. What activities are coming up in the next week where you can practise some of your new-found tools and techniques? If nothing comes immediately to mind what opportunities can you create? Remember presenting yourself with impact is not just about large, formal presentations; it could simply be an opportunity to present your ideas in a different way at a meeting. Commit to doing something now. Send out a meeting invitation. Ask to present a specific agenda item at a forthcoming meeting. Arrange to present your ideas to date on a specific project at a meeting you are arranging. It does not have to be a large event. Think about baby steps. What can you do, right now? When you have got some ideas, take steps to create momentum. This may put you outside your comfort zone and it will be a great way of learning.

## REHEARSE AND REFLECT

Having thought about your learning style, you may have concluded that your Reflector style could be further enhanced. That you tend to rush into things without adequate preparation and thought for the possible consequences. You may also find it difficult to make time to pause and review experiences/identify lessons learned.

Many years ago I took my NLP Master Practitioner qualification. As part of this qualification we all had to undertake a modelling project. We were encouraged to select a topic on the basis that this particular skill or ability was something that we felt we wanted to be better at. We were encouraged to identify exemplars, people who were particularly good at doing the skill we had identified, and to meet with them and discover the essence of how they did what they did. One of my colleagues was on the same workshop as me and she chose 'Getting Engaged in 30 seconds' as her topic. She believed that she was not particularly skilful at making an immediate impact with her audience and wanted to improve in this area.

My colleague selected a number of people whom she had heard present and, who she believed, had the ability to just present and engage with their audience without preparation and notes. However, as she started to interview her exemplars an interesting pattern emerged.

One of her exemplars had been a former work colleague. My colleague vividly recalled his leaving speech delivered to a couple of hundred people one afternoon. It was in her words, "spontaneous and totally off the cuff". Yet, when she spoke to her former colleague, he recalled how he had been unable to sleep the night before as he had been so busy rehearsing what he was going to say. The same was true of all her exemplars. They had all delivered what had appeared to be spontaneous and off the cuff presentations. Nevertheless, all were underpinned by hours of preparation and rehearsal.

Recently another colleague volunteered that her mantra for delivering an excellent presentation is *prepare, prepare, prepare!* She says she ensures that she knows her slides "110%", she prepares and rehearses her introduction so she knows this word perfect and leaves as little to chance as possible. She even decides if, asked, "Would you like a drink?" what drink she will have!

On reflection the above anecdotes are probably not that surprising. Presenting is after all a skill and we become proficient at a skill by practising. Consider David Beckham or Ronaldo taking a free kick. Their technique looks effortless. Yet Alex Ferguson recounts stories of both of them practising hour after hour, long after their team mates had left the training ground, to perfect that swerve, the flight of the ball. Think about some of the more recent great presentations you have witnessed, be it David Cameron at the Annual Conservative Party Convention in 2008, delivering his speech without notes or autocue, or one of President Obama's many speeches. Natural and spontaneous as they may appear, there were all almost certainly honed and perfected through hours of practise. There really are no short cuts to excellence.

Therefore, having written your presentation, prepared your slides and visual aids take some time to practise. Stand in front of a mirror and observe how you look.

Practise projecting your voice, particularly if you are going to be presenting in a large room. Time your presentation so you know how long it takes.

Once you have delivered your presentation, you may be feeling that your job is done. Not quite. There is one important aspect that I would encourage you to spend some time on before you move on to the next task – reflection. Having given a presentation, be it at a workshop or at a coaching session, I always spend time on reflection and feedback. Indeed we often spend longer on this part than it took to deliver the actual presentation. Feedback and reflection are vital as these allow us to learn from an event, consider that learning and plan how to do things differently in the future. When running a feedback session I always start with the individual who has just presented, before inviting comments from others.

So, having delivered your presentation, I would encourage you to spend some time answering the following questions:

- What went well? What aspects of your presentation were you pleased with?
- What could you have done better and/or differently?
- What did you learn from this experience?
- What are you going to do differently next time?

If you have a recording of your presentation, so much the better. Watch your presentation again with a critical eye. Observe what you did well as well as what you could have done differently or better.

Having spent some time reflecting on the above I would also encourage you to get **feedback** from others. Remember giving feedback is a skill and not everyone will be versed in giving focused, specific feedback that you can do something with. It may therefore be useful to prime colleagues/friends in advance on what exactly you would like feedback on. For example, if you are concentrating on making a really powerful first impression, it would be useful for your colleagues/friends to know this in advance so that they can give you feedback on this aspect of your presentation. At the end of this chapter you will find the presentation feedback form that I use at workshops and with coaching clients. I find this useful in getting really specific feedback.

## CONCLUDING FROM YOUR EXPERIENCE

If, at the start of this chapter, you concluded that for you the Theorist style could be strengthened, chances are you regard theories, frameworks and models as being rather academic and esoteric. You probably found the hints and tips and real life examples more interesting than some of the frameworks and models. You may also take things at face value, jump to quick conclusions and prefer short term tactics to a longer-term approach.

If this is the case I would encourage you to put aside some time and adopt a more rational and analytical approach to reviewing your performance. In your opinion what is going well for you? What improvements have you noticed? What have you tried so far? What successes have you had? Take some time to note down accurately what is working for you at the moment. Only then turn to what could have gone better. Be as specific as you can in giving yourself feedback. Really concentrate on the one or two things that have emerged as consistent pieces of feedback, either from yourself or from others. Give yourself a score on a scale of one to ten, ten being the highest score. Having given yourself a score make sure this score is in line with the feedback you have just reviewed. If, for example, you gave yourself seven out of ten, ask yourself "What would make it ten?" Really focus on the specific things that you could have done more of, or done differently, to take your presentation from good to excellent. Challenge yourself to think about how else you can use some of the tools and techniques in this book. Ask yourself what other tools and techniques you could use. Practise the "what if?" question.

## NEXT STEPS

If you concluded that your Pragmatist style could be enhanced, you probably find that you hanker after perfect solutions to problems rather than settling for something practical and less elegant. Similarly, you may be wary of specific plans and actions that commit you to deliverables and target dates. If this is the case I would encourage you to resist critiquing the ideas, theories and techniques in this book and simply try some of them out to see if they work for you. In workshops or coaching sessions I often find myself saying "You will never know if something will work for you or not unless you have a go!" And I passionately believe that. Challenge yourself to be open to new ideas about presenting yourself and be prepared to tailor-make them for your circumstances.

Finally, remind yourself that learning is an ongoing process. Once you have reflected on your performance in one situation, spend some time thinking about a future event and how you can put some of your ideas into practice. Remember practise, practise, practise!

## PRESENTING YOURSELF WITH IMPACT CHECKLIST

Congratulations! You now have all the tools you need to present yourself with impact. Here is a quick checklist to remind you.

❏ What is your desired outcome? (See Chapter 1)

❏ What enabling beliefs do you need to make use of? (See Chapter 2)

❏ Step into your audience's shoes to decide on your message. (See Chapter 8)

❏ Decide how you are going to build rapport. (See Chapter 3)

❏ Decide how you are going to engage all the senses. (See Chapter 4)

❏ Decide what language patterns you will use. (See Chapter 5)

❏ Plan the presentation, decide on props and tools, rehearse, and get feedback. (See Chapter 9)

❏ On the day. Set up as early as you can. Use a resourceful state. (See Chapter 6)

❏ During the presentation use your whole mind and body. (See Chapter 7)

❏ Get feedback and reflect on how you can present with even more impact. (See Chapter 10)

# FOOD FOR THOUGHT: THE FLOCK OF SEAGULLS

There was a flock of seagulls living on the coast and they would happily go about their daily business by walking everywhere: to the shops, to school, to work, down to the pub.

One day a young seagull was in the village square when a mild breeze ruffled his wing feathers. He thought "That was nice!" He decided to do it again and this time the breeze was a little stronger and it lifted him off his feet. He flapped his wings in panic trying to get back to the ground. Well, what do you think happened? He took off towards the skies. Once his initial panic subsided he began to experiment with his newly found skill. He began to do loop-the-loops, death dives, spirals and all manner of aerobatic activities. Above all, he liked it. He was laughing. He felt happy inside and he decided to share this with the rest of the flock. He came back down and landed, very gently, in the village square. He rang the church bell, which was the flock's method of getting everyone together for important announcements. All the other seagulls left their houses, schools and workplaces and walked into the square wondering why the church bell had summoned them.

"Watch this," the young gull said, "It's absolutely brilliant!" He flapped his wings and took-off. He gave a fantastic aerial display and landed back in the square. "Try it, guys; it really is the most fantastic experience!"

After a short period of indecision one of the elder gulls flapped his wings and took-off. Very soon the skies were filled with laughing seagulls. They were buzzing each other, pretending to be bomber-planes, loop-the-looping, spiralling and generally enjoying themselves in a way they had never before experienced.

After a few hours they all landed back in the square. They were giggling with each other. "Did you see me do that death dive? How about when I nearly hit you mid-air? What a great roll that was", and so on. They were in a fantastic mood and were all delighted with their new-found skills.

Do you know what they did next? They all walked home!

This is one of my favourite training stories and I often tell it at the end of a workshop. In a light-hearted way it begs the question, "How often do we spend time and effort learning new skills or techniques, only to continue doing exactly the same as we have always done?"

So, now that you have found your wings, keep on flying!

# APPENDIX

## PRESENTING YOURSELF WITH IMPACT FEEDBACK FORM

Presenter's Name: _____

Your Name: _____

### IN YOUR OPINION TO WHAT EXTENT DID THE PRESENTER:

- Present in a way that was compelling and interesting to watch?

- Build rapport with you/their audience? If so how?

- Use enriched language (see, hear, feel)

- Use influential language patterns

- Invite you to 'participate' in the experience?

### WHAT I LIKED WAS...

### WHAT I'D LIKE MORE OF IS...

# BIBLIOGRAPHY

Borg, J (2007) *Persuasion – The art of influencing people*, Pearson. ISBN 978-0-27371299-2

Cialdini, R.B. (2007) *Influence - The Psychology of Persuasion*, Collins. ISBN 978-0-06124189-5

Cooper, L. (2008) *Business NLP for Dummies*, John Wiley. ISBN 978-0-47069757-3

Honey, P. and Mumford, A. (1992) *The Manual of Learning Styles*, Peter Honey. ISBN 978-0-95084447-3

James, T. and Shephard, D. (2004) *Presenting Magically*, Crown House Publishing. ISBN 978-1-89983652-9

Knight, S. (2002) *NLP at Work*, Nicholas Brealey. ISBN 978-1-85788302-2

Laborde, G.Z. (2003) *Influencing with Integrity*, Crown House Publishing Ltd. ISBN 978-0-93334710-6

O'Connor, J. and Seymour, J. (1994) *Training with NLP*, Thorsons. ISBN 0-7225-2853-1

Zelazny, G. (2006) *Say it with Presentations*, McGraw Hill. ISBN 0-07-147289-4

Other resources are available from
*www.iridiumconsulting.co.uk/links.html*

You may also like to sign up now for Gill's monthly hints and tips newsletter at
*www.iridiumconsulting.co.uk/links.html*

# GILL GRAVES MA, MBA, FCIPD

Gill is an experienced executive coach and consultant in leadership and team development focused on enabling individuals and organisations to achieve their goals and realise their full potential. Gill is a recognised leader in the field of business communications skills and their practical applications.

**Education:** Gill has an MA in Coaching and Mentoring, an MBA from Warwick University and a degree in English. She is a fellow of the CIPD. She is also an NLP Master Practitioner and NLP Trainer and certified to use a range of psychometric instruments including the Myers Briggs Type Indicator, Emotional Competence Inventory and OPQ32.

**Work Experience:** Formerly Human Resources Director for Europe and Asia of a US high tech company, Gill has extensive hands-on international human resources, organisational development, training and coaching experience, gained within multi-cultural, multi-national, fast-growing, rapidly changing environments.

Gill founded Iridium (*www.iridiumconsulting.co.uk*) in May 2000 with a mission to help companies recruit, develop and retain their most important assets – their people.

**Coaching and Facilitation Experience:** Gill works with major corporations in the UK and abroad including Vodafone, the Open University, CASS Business School, BAE Systems and the NHS. Gill's work incorporates development of individuals, teams and leaders, both one to one and in groups.

Email her at: gill@iridiumconsulting.co.uk

discovering your talent

# PRESENTING
# YOURSELF
WITH
# IMPACT
## MASTERCLASS
## WITH GILL GRAVES

No matter how skilled you are in your particular line of work, it is your ability to communicate with and influence others that will do much to determine your level of professional success. Traditional communication theory has been based on the medium and form of the message, and of late, on the technology.

By contrast, this Masterclass will focus on how you present the whole of you, formally and informally. We will concentrate on your non verbal communication, the language you use, how you use your physiology and how you establish and maintain presence. It is NOT a PowerPoint training course – in fact using PowerPoint will be highly optional.

Workshop Objectives - You will learn how to:

- ✓ Use the technique of "Starting with the end in mind" to prepare for future meetings, presentations and negotiations to ensure that there is a clear outcome in mind.
- ✓ Understand and try on the beliefs of people who consistently present themselves with impact.
- ✓ Manage yourself so that you can achieve a state of energy, resourcefulness and confidence whenever you choose.
- ✓ Deliver a recorded presentation that is enriching, in both style and content.
- ✓ Understand the concept of "enriched language" and how this can be used to really "sell" ideas to a diverse group of people.
- ✓ Appreciate the power of language – exploring language of influence.
- ✓ Understand the true impact of your communication – your words, your non verbal communication, your stance, your posture.
- ✓ Structure your message so that it meets the needs of your audience.
- ✓ Determine your next steps to embed your learning from the workshop.

This Masterclass is generally run as an in-house programme. There are also a limited number of open Masterclasses each year. Contact Gill now...

**www.iridiumconsulting.co.uk**

Also available from Bookshaker.com

*Proven Psychological*
*Secrets to Help You*
*Beat The Office Bully*

*Dr. Scott's*

# Verbal
# Self
# Defense
*in*
## The Workplace

Dr. Daniel Scott

Lightning Source UK Ltd.
Milton Keynes UK
UKOW06f2138090516

273904UK00001B/1/P